THE ULTIMATE HANDBOOK TO

COMPANION PLANTING

FOR BEGINNERS

JEFF TUCKER

First published in 2024 by Jeff Tucker Homesteading Press, in the United Kingdom.

https://www.facebook.com/groups/jefftuckerhomesteading
ISBN: 9781068575501

A CIP catalogue record for this book is available from the British Library.

Typeset by Jeff Tucker Homesteading Press.

Cover art and design by Jeff Tucker Homesteading Press.

Dedicated to all of the aspiring and journeying gardeners of the
world who understand that plants, much like people,
do better in company.

Introduction

HELLO, FELLOW GARDENER!

From the sweet scent of freshly turned earth to the joy of harvesting your own sun-ripened tomatoes, there's something undeniably rewarding about tending a garden. My journey into the world of gardening began many moons ago on the fertile plots of my grandad's allotment. There, amid rows of bustling greenery, I stumbled upon a simple truth that would shape my gardening philosophy: plants, like people, thrive in good company.

I remember one fresh Spring morning—I was about ten—helping Grandad plant marigolds among his tomatoes. He explained that these bright flowers weren't just for show; they helped keep the aphids away. That day sparked my fascination with companion planting, a method that uses the natural affinities between plants to enhance growth, deter pests, and ensure a bountiful harvest.

This book, "The Ultimate Handbook to Companion Planting for Beginners," is crafted with you, the beginner gardener, in mind. My aim is simple: to equip you with the knowledge and confidence to implement companion planting in your own garden, using methods that are as natural as they are effective. Whether you dream of lush vegetable beds, fragrant herb patches, or vibrant fruit orchards, this guide is your first step towards a thriving garden, cultivated with care and devoid of chemicals.

Companion planting offers numerous benefits, not the least of which include boosting your garden's yield and fostering a healthier ecosystem right in your backyard. By understanding which plants benefit each other, you can naturally repel pests, improve soil health, and create a more resilient garden.

This book is structured to be both informative and easy to navigate. It provides detailed discussions of companion plants alongside practical tips for garden setup, maintenance, and organic pest control. You will find yourself returning to these pages often, each time discovering new insights to apply to your ever-growing garden.

What sets this handbook apart is its focus on simplicity and effectiveness, particularly for those new to gardening. The extensive lists of plant pairings are designed to serve as a quick reference to help you make the best choices for your garden's unique needs. Coupled with a steadfast avoidance of synthetic chemicals, this book embraces a pure, back-to-basics approach to gardening that anyone can follow.

So, I invite you to roll up your sleeves and join me in the rewarding practice of companion planting. With a bit of patience and this book in hand, you are well on your way to cultivating a garden that is not only productive but also a vibrant ecosystem in its own right.

Let's grow together!

—JEFF TUCKER

Chapter 1:
Understanding the Basics of Companion Planting

A S YOU STEP INTO THE gardening world, I want you to think of it like entering a bustling city where every plant plays a role in the community's well-being. Now, let me share a little story that might just change how you view your garden forever. Many years ago, I visited an old friend who practiced what seemed like magical gardening. In his vegetable plot, tomatoes were flanked by aromatic basil, and marigolds spread cheerfully around. This wasn't just for beauty; he explained that basil helped enhance the tomato's flavor while marigolds kept pests at bay. This simple yet effective strategy is what companion planting is all about—a practice where different plants are strategically placed together to support each other's growth and health. This chapter will explore the foundational concepts of companion planting, helping you understand how to harness these relationships to create a flourishing garden.

1.1 Harmony in the Garden

Companion planting is not a new fad; it's a practice deeply rooted in observing nature. In natural ecosystems, plants, animals, and microorganisms live together in a balance that promotes the health and productivity of the community. By mimicking these relationships in your garden, you can create a harmonious environment where plants support each other. For instance, tall sunflowers provide shade for heat-sensitive lettuce, while the lettuce at their feet can help keep the soil moist for the sunflowers' benefit. This mutual support system reduces plant stress, allowing them to thrive.

Mutual Benefits Explained

The benefits of companion planting are extensive and varied. At its core, this practice is about understanding and utilizing the natural synergies between different plants. Some plants, like beans, fix nitrogen in the soil, which helps nitrogen-loving plants like corn grow better. Others, like garlic, release substances that repel garden pests, protecting more vulnerable plant neighbors. Then there are plants like onions, whose strong scent can mask the aroma of nearby carrots, thus throwing off carrot flies. By pairing plants that offer mutual benefits, you optimize your garden's health and yield.

History and Cultural Significance

Tracing the roots of companion planting leads us back through centuries and across continents. Indigenous tribes in the Americas famously practiced the "Three Sisters" method, where corn, beans, and squash were grown together, each plant offering something to aid the others. Corn provides a structure for the beans to climb, beans fix nitrogen in the soil beneficial for corn and squash, and squash spreads its leaves to shade the soil, keeping it moist and weed-free. This method showcases how ancient cultures utilized companion planting principles to enhance agricultural productivity long before modern gardening tools and techniques were developed.

Sustainability at its Core

In modern times, the importance of sustainable practices has never been more pronounced, and companion planting fits perfectly into this ethos. By optimizing natural plant interactions, gardeners can significantly reduce their reliance on chemical fertilizers, pesticides, and excessive water use. For example, strategically placing pest-repelling plants can diminish the need for chemical sprays, while dense planting can reduce water evaporation from the soil. Thus, companion planting supports your garden's ecosystem and promotes a healthier, more sustainable approach to gardening.

Interactive Element: Reflection Section

Consider your current garden setup or the one you envision. Are there plants you could group together based on the mutual benefits they offer each other? Take a moment to jot down a few pairs of plants you believe could thrive side-by-side. This exercise will help you start thinking like a companion planter, recognizing relationships that could transform your garden.

1.2 Decoding the Language of Plants: Key Terms and Concepts

As we delve deeper into the world of companion planting, understanding the terminology and concepts is like learning a new language—the language of plants. This knowledge is not just academic; it's practical and can profoundly affect the health and productivity of your garden. Let's start with some key terms that form the bedrock of companion planting.

Basic Terminology

Knowing the specific jargon in every field can open doors to deeper understanding and more effective practices. In companion planting, terms such as "nitrogen fixers," "pollinators," and "cover crops" are frequently used. Nitrogen fixers are plants that have a unique ability to convert atmospheric nitrogen into a form that is usable by plants. This group includes legumes like peas and beans, which, through a symbiotic relationship with bacteria in their root nodules, enrich the soil with nitrogen, benefiting neighboring plants. Pollinators, on the other hand, are creatures like bees, butterflies, and birds that transfer pollen from one flower to another, facilitating plant reproduction. Gardens that attract pollinators are often more productive and have better fruiting. Lastly, cover crops are planted primarily to manage soil erosion, improve soil health, and maintain ecological balance, even when not intended for harvest. These might include crops like clover or rye, which protect and enrich the soil.

Understanding Plant Needs

Every plant in your garden has its own requirements and ways of communicating these needs. Basic needs like sunlight, water, and nutrients are well known, but understanding how plants interact with their environment can significantly enhance your gardening practice. For example, a plant wilting might indicate a lack of water but could also suggest root problems or a soilborne disease. Similarly, the color of the leaves can tell you a great deal about nutrient deficiencies; yellow leaves often indicate a lack of nitrogen. When you start to see your plants as living entities with ways of communicating, you're better equipped to meet their needs and manage your garden more effectively.

The Science of Plant Interactions

The interactions between different plants in your garden can have a substantial impact on their growth and viability. Scientific studies have shown that certain plant combinations have mutually beneficial relationships, often referred to as positive allelopathy. For instance, the exudates from marigold roots can repel nematodes in the soil, which might otherwise harm susceptible plants like tomatoes. Understanding these interactions allows gardeners to strategically place plants in a way that naturally enhances growth and health. This knowledge of plant science not only helps in creating a more productive garden but also minimizes the need for chemical interventions.

Companion vs. Antagonist Plants

Just as some plants perform better when near certain others, some combinations can be detrimental, known as antagonistic relationships. For instance, while beans thrive when planted with marigolds, they may suffer when placed too close to onions or garlic, which can inhibit their growth. This concept of antagonism is crucial in planning your garden layout. It's about more than just understanding who gets along; it's about preventing relationships that could hinder your garden's productivity. Recognizing which plants are companions and which are antagonists can save you from unforeseen gardening challenges, ensuring that each plant can grow without negative interference from its neighbors.

By integrating these concepts and terms into your gardening practice, you're not just throwing seeds in the soil and hoping for the best. You're strategically orchestrating a community of plants that can support and enhance each other's growth. This informed approach makes your garden a visually stunning display and a testament to the functionality and intelligence of nature-inspired planting.

1.3 How Companion Planting Contributes to Sustainability

One of the most compelling aspects of companion planting is its ability to significantly reduce the reliance on chemical inputs, such as fertilizers and pesticides, that are commonly used in conventional gardening. By carefully selecting plant pairs that naturally complement each other, you can create a garden that thrives and supports a healthier ecosystem. For example, consider the classic pairing of corn and beans, which is more than just a staple in many diets. In this duo, beans, as legumes, have the ability to fix atmospheric nitrogen into the soil, enriching it and providing the necessary nutrients for corn, which is a heavy feeder of nitrogen. This natural process reduces the need for synthetic nitrogen fertilizers, which are often derived from non-renewable resources and can cause environmental harm such as water pollution and greenhouse gas emissions.

Moreover, companion planting can significantly reduce the use of chemical pesticides. Plants like marigolds, nasturtiums, and chrysanthemums can deter pests through naturally occurring compounds that repel unwanted insects or attract beneficial predators like ladybugs and lacewings. By integrating these plants into your garden, you create a natural defense system that reduces the need for harmful pesticides. This approach not only preserves the local insect population but also ensures that fruits and vegetables are free from chemical residues, making them healthier for consumption.

Enhancing soil health is yet another vital benefit of companion planting. When plants like deep-rooted vegetables are paired with shallow-rooted herbs, they can help break up the soil without mechanical intervention, improving aeration and drainage. Additionally, some companion plants act as living mulches— spreading out to cover the soil, retaining moisture, and suppressing weeds, which reduces the need for frequent watering and the application of herbicides. These living mulches also contribute organic matter as they decompose, which enhances soil structure and fertility. This dynamic process not only nurtures the plants but also supports various soil organisms, from bacteria to earthworms, playing a crucial role in the decomposition process and nutrient cycling.

Water conservation is equally crucial and is adeptly supported by companion planting strategies. Strategic plant pairings can significantly improve water efficiency in the garden. For instance, taller plants can provide shade to smaller, more heat-sensitive plants, reducing water evaporation from the soil surface and thereby decreasing the water needed for irrigation. This method of natural shading can be particularly beneficial during the peak of summer when water can become a scarce resource. Furthermore, plants with different root depths, when planted together, ensure optimal use of water, as they extract moisture from different soil layers, which minimizes water waste and maximizes water usage efficiency.

Promoting biodiversity in the garden is another sustainable advantage of companion planting. By diversifying the plant species in a garden, you can create a habitat that supports a wide range of wildlife and beneficial insects. This biodiversity is not only crucial for ecological health but also enhances the beauty and interest of your garden space. Diverse plantings can attract pollinators such as bees and butterflies, which are essential for the pollination of many crops. Additionally, a variety of plants can provide habitats and food sources for various creatures, which can help maintain ecological balance and prevent any one pest species from becoming overwhelming.

In summary, companion planting offers a multifaceted approach to gardening that aligns with the principles of sustainability. It reduces the need for chemical inputs, enhances soil health, conserves water, and promotes biodiversity. Each of these factors plays a crucial role in creating a garden that is not only productive but also sustainable and environmentally friendly. As you integrate these practices into your gardening, you'll find that companion planting is more than just a technique—it's a philosophy that enriches both the garden and the gardener.

1.4 The Role of Biodiversity in Your Garden

Within the verdant bounds of a meticulously cared-for garden, the subtle nuances of biodiversity narrate a story of vitality and ecological harmony. Envision wandering into a garden where every plant not only elevates the aesthetic charm but also plays a pivotal role in nurturing a vibrant ecosystem. This is the core principle behind encouraging biodiversity in your garden—an approach that involves weaving together a diverse tapestry of plant life to unlock an array of benefits, ranging from improved pollination to effective natural pest management.

Ecosystem Services

A biodiverse garden is a powerhouse of ecosystem services. For instance, consider the role of flowering plants such as lavender and cosmos. These are not only pleasing to the eye but are crucial in attracting pollinators like bees and butterflies. Pollination is essential for the production of fruits and seeds and is a critical service for ensuring food diversity and security. Furthermore, plants such as dill and fennel attract beneficial insects, including wasps and ladybugs, which naturally manage pest populations by preying on common garden pests such as aphids and caterpillars. Thus, incorporating a diverse range of plants can reduce the need for chemical pesticides, which not only preserves the local wildlife but also maintains the ecological balance, ensuring that your garden remains a self-regulating system.

Resilience through Diversity

Diversity in a garden introduces a variety of traits that plants have evolved over millennia to withstand fluctuations and adversities in their environments. This variability is what makes a garden resilient. For example, some plants are more drought-resistant, while others can thrive in damper soils. By cultivating a mix of these plants, your garden can better withstand unpredictable weather patterns, whether it's a sudden drought or excessive rainfall. Moreover, a diversity of plants can prevent the spread of disease and pest infestations. If one plant species is affected, it is less likely to impact the entire garden, as different plants often have different susceptibilities. This natural form of risk management is invaluable in maintaining a healthy garden.

Attracting Beneficial Wildlife

The inclusion of diverse plant species in your garden does more than just beautify the space; it turns it into a sanctuary for beneficial wildlife. Each plant type emits unique signals through its flowers, leaves, and roots that can attract a specific group of beneficial insects or animals. For instance, the bright flowers of sunflowers can attract birds that not only add life to your garden but also help in controlling insect populations by feeding on them. Similarly, the presence of certain herbs like mint and basil can deter unwanted pests while attracting pollinators. Creating such a habitat encourages these natural allies to take up residence in your garden, thereby supporting your plants' health and growth.

Cultural and Visual Diversity

Integrating a wide array of plants enhances the cultural and aesthetic appeal of your garden. Each plant brings its own story, its own connection to a particular heritage or tradition. For example, planting marigolds might remind someone of traditional Indian weddings, which use these flowers extensively, or of the Mexican Day of the Dead celebrations. Similarly, a patch of lavender can evoke memories of French countryside gardens. These plants do more than serve ecological functions; they connect us to different cultures and histories, enriching our garden experience. Additionally, the visual diversity plants offer—from the varying colors and textures of their leaves to the distinct shapes and sizes of their blooms—provides a daily spectacle that changes with the seasons, offering continual delight and discovery.

In your own garden, the integration of various plant species not only promotes a robust ecosystem but also transforms your garden into a dynamic environment enriched with ecological benefits, resilience, and beauty. This approach not only enhances the functionality and sustainability of your garden but also provides a richer, more engaging gardening experience. As you plant and nurture a diverse array of species, you contribute to a larger ecological tapestry that supports life in myriad forms. The simple act of gardening becomes a powerful gesture toward sustaining the natural world, offering refuge and resources to a wide range of organisms. In doing so, you step into a relationship with the natural world that is deeply reciprocal, one where beauty and utility are intertwined in the dance of life.

Chapter 2:
Preparing Your Garden

A S THE SUN CASTS ITS early morning glow across the dew-freshened landscape, imagine stepping into a space that's been perfectly crafted for both beauty and productivity. Creating such a space begins long before the first seed is sown; it starts with thoughtful preparation of your garden's foundation—the very earth that will cradle and nurture your plants. In this chapter, we delve into the initial yet crucial steps you must consider to lay the groundwork for a successful companion garden. Selecting the right location for your garden is much like choosing a home; it requires careful consideration of various environmental factors that will affect the growth and health of your plants.

2.1 Choosing the Right Location for Your Companion Garden

Assessing Sunlight and Shade

Light is the lifeblood of your garden. Each plant in your future green haven will have its specific sunlight needs, ranging from full sun to partial shade. Observing how sunlight plays across your potential garden site throughout the day is vital. You might notice that some areas bask in continuous sunlight while others lie in partial or full shade. This pattern is crucial for deciding where each plant will thrive best. For instance, vegetables like tomatoes and peppers adore the sun and require at least six to eight hours of direct sunlight daily to flourish. In contrast, leafy greens such as spinach and some herbs prefer cooler, shadier spots. By understanding these patterns, you can strategically place plants in positions that meet their sunlight requirements, ensuring they grow vigorously and healthily.

Soil Type Considerations

The type of soil in your garden is not just dirt; it's a complex ecosystem that provides nutrients, aeration, and moisture to your plants. Before deciding on the location of your garden, it's essential to determine the soil type. Is it clay, sandy, loamy, or chalky? Each type has its characteristics and challenges. For example, clay soils are nutrient-rich but slow to drain and can become waterlogged. Sandy soils, on the other hand, are quick to drain but do not hold nutrients well. Loamy soil, a balanced mix of sand, silt, and clay, is ideal for most plants. Understanding your soil type will help you choose not only the right plants but also the amendments needed to create the perfect growing environment.

Water Access and Drainage

Water is another critical factor in the health of your garden. When choosing your garden's location, consider both access to water and natural drainage. Your garden should be close enough to a water source to make watering convenient, yet it should also be capable of draining excess water effectively. Poor drainage can lead to waterlogged soil, which can suffocate plant roots and lead to rot. If drainage is a concern, consider raised beds or amend the soil with organic matter to improve its structure. Conversely, if the area is too dry, strategies such as mulching or installing a simple irrigation system might be necessary.

Space Planning

The amount of space available can significantly influence the design of your garden. If you're limited in space, don't be discouraged. Many effective gardening techniques can maximize your growing area. Vertical gardening, for example, is an excellent solution for small spaces. Cucumbers, tomatoes, and even some varieties of squash can be trained to grow upwards on trellises or supports, significantly reducing their footprint. Container gardening is another versatile option that allows you to grow plants on patios, balconies, or even windowsills. Containers can be moved to take advantage of the best sunlight and can be filled with high-quality soil tailored to the needs of specific plants.

Interactive Element: Sunlight Assessment Exercise

To help you understand your garden's lighting conditions better, here's a simple exercise: Observe and record the amount of sunlight different areas in your potential garden space receive throughout the day. Do this observation several times over a few days to get an accurate understanding. Note the hours of full sun and shade, and use this information to sketch a preliminary map of where specific plants might thrive best according to their light requirements. This exercise will not only aid in effective plant placement but also deepen your connection with the natural dynamics of your garden space.

In preparing your garden, every decision you make—from selecting the right location to understanding the intricacies of soil and water—lays the foundation for a thriving companion planting system. These initial steps are vital in ensuring that your garden is not only a place of beauty and productivity but also a testament to thoughtful, sustainable gardening practices. As you step forward with these preparations, remember that each choice is a step towards creating a vibrant, life-supporting oasis that will bring joy and harvest for seasons to come.

2.2 Soil Preparation and Improvement Techniques

In the heart of every flourishing garden lies the soil, a dynamic and living ecosystem that plays a crucial role in the health and productivity of your plants. Preparing and improving your garden soil is not just about digging and planting; it involves understanding and enhancing the soil's structure, fertility, and life-supporting capabilities. Let's explore some essential techniques to prepare and enrich your garden's soil, ensuring it becomes a thriving foundation for your plants.

Testing Soil Health

Before making any amendments, it's essential to assess the current state of your soil. This means testing for two key aspects: fertility and pH level. Soil fertility tests measure nutrient levels, including nitrogen, phosphorus, and potassium, which are critical for plant health. A simple soil test kit, available at most garden centers, can provide this information. Additionally, testing the soil's pH—a measure of how acidic or alkaline it is—can help you understand which plants will thrive in your garden and which amendments may be needed to optimize conditions for growth. For instance, if your soil is too acidic, incorporating lime can help neutralize it, whereas sulfur may be needed to acidify alkaline soils. These tests not only guide your amendment choices but also help you understand the natural tendencies of your garden's environment, allowing you to select plants that are best suited to your soil conditions.

Organic Matter Enrichment

One of the most effective ways to improve soil health is by adding organic matter. This includes compost, green manure, and other decomposable materials like leaf mold or aged manure. Adding organic matter improves soil structure, which enhances its ability to hold water and nutrients. It also encourages the activity of beneficial microorganisms, which play a key role in breaking down organic material into nutrients that plants can absorb. For instance, compost made from kitchen scraps and yard waste provides a rich, balanced mix of nutrients that can significantly boost your soil's fertility. Green manures—fast-growing plants sown to cover bare soil and later turned under—add nutrients back into the soil while improving its structure. Regularly incorporating organic matter into your garden soil not only nourishes the plants but also keeps the soil alive and responsive, creating an environment where plants can flourish.

Natural Fertilizers

While organic matter provides a broad spectrum of nutrients, targeted applications of natural fertilizers can address specific nutritional needs or deficiencies. Natural fertilizers, such as bone meal, blood meal, or fish emulsion, offer concentrated sources of essential nutrients like phosphorus, nitrogen, and potassium. These fertilizers release nutrients slowly, reducing the risk of over-fertilization and providing a steady supply of nutrition to your plants throughout the growing season. When applying natural fertilizers, it's important to follow recommended rates and methods to avoid overwhelming your plants and soil. For example, applying a nitrogen-rich blood meal to leafy vegetables can enhance their growth and vigor, while phosphorus-rich bone meal is excellent for promoting healthy root development in flowering plants and vegetables.

Creating a Living Soil

The concept of 'living soil' refers to soil rich in organic matter and teeming with microbial life, both of which are critical for sustaining plant health. This vibrant soil ecosystem is achieved not only through the addition of organic matter and natural fertilizers but also through practices that support soil life. Avoiding the use of chemical pesticides and fertilizers, which can disrupt soil microbiology, is crucial. Instead, focus on fostering a diverse soil environment through crop rotation, cover cropping, and reduced tillage, which help maintain a healthy balance of nutrients and organic matter. Encouraging a rich soil life enhances plant health naturally, reducing the need for chemical inputs and creating a garden that is both productive and sustainable.

By integrating these soil preparation and improvement techniques, you ensure your garden has a strong and vibrant foundation. Properly nourished and balanced soil not only supports the growth of robust plants but also enhances their ability to withstand pests and diseases, making your gardening efforts more successful and rewarding. As you tend to your soil, remember that you are nurturing a living ecosystem that, in turn, will nurture your plants, creating a harmonious and thriving garden.

2.3 Understanding the Importance of Sunlight and Watering

Sunlight is akin to a symphony conductor for your garden, orchestrating the growth and health of your plants through its daily patterns. Each type of plant in your garden ensemble has unique needs when it comes to light exposure. For example, fruit-bearing plants such as tomatoes and peppers thrive under full sunlight, which catalyzes the photosynthesis process vital for their growth and fruit production. On the other hand, plants like lettuce and cilantro might require less intense light, preferring the cool shelter provided by partial shade, especially in hotter climates. Positioning your plants according to their light requirements is crucial and involves observing the path of sunlight across your garden throughout the day. This observation helps you understand which areas receive full sun, partial shade, or full shade. With this knowledge, you can strategically place your sun-loving plants in areas where they receive ample light throughout the day while reserving shaded spots for those that require protection from intense midday sun. This thoughtful placement ensures that each plant gets its ideal amount of sunlight, leading to healthier growth and more bountiful yields.

Watering your garden effectively is another cornerstone of successful gardening, particularly in companion planting setups where different plants with varying water needs coexist closely. Efficient watering techniques ensure that each plant receives the right amount of water without wastage or overwatering, which can be detrimental to plant health. One effective technique is the use of soaker hoses or drip irrigation systems, which deliver water directly to the base of the plants, minimizing evaporation and ensuring that water goes where it's most needed — the roots. These methods are especially beneficial in companion planting, as they allow for targeted watering that can be adjusted according to the specific needs of each plant grouping. For instance, leafy greens, which may require consistent moisture, can be watered more frequently, while herbs that thrive in drier conditions can be watered less often. This method not only conserves water but also prevents the spread of leaf diseases that can occur when foliage remains wet for extended periods.

Mulching plays a pivotal role in moisture conservation, a key aspect of maintaining a healthy garden. Organic mulches such as straw, bark, or shredded leaves not only suppress weeds but also help retain soil moisture, reducing the need for frequent watering. By covering the soil, mulch reduces evaporation, keeping the soil cool and moist longer. This is particularly advantageous during hot weather when water can evaporate quickly from the soil surface. Furthermore, as organic mulch slowly decomposes, it adds valuable organic matter back into the soil, enhancing its structure and fertility. Mulching is a simple yet effective practice that supports water conservation and soil health, ultimately fostering more robust plant growth. In a companion planting garden, where diverse plant species coexist, mulching also helps create a uniform environment that can balance the different moisture needs of various plants, aiding in the overall harmony and productivity of the garden.

Exploring the different irrigation systems available can greatly enhance your garden's efficiency and yield. Beyond soaker hoses and drip systems, more sophisticated options like automated drip irrigation can be tailored to the specific needs of your garden. These systems can be set up with timers and adjusted to water certain sections of your garden more frequently than others based on the individual water needs of different plants. For gardeners looking to optimize their watering schedule and conserve water, an automated system can be invaluable. It eliminates the guesswork and manual labor involved in watering, ensuring that plants receive the precise amount of water at optimal times, which is especially crucial in a companion planting setup where plant interactions are complex. Whether you choose a simple manual method or a high-tech automated system, the right irrigation setup can make a substantial difference in the health and productivity of your garden, allowing you to grow a lush, vibrant companion planting garden with less effort and more joy.

2.4 Designing Your Companion Planting Layout

When you begin to design your garden, it's like sketching a blueprint that will guide the flourishing of your plants. The layout of your garden is not just about aesthetics; it's a strategic plan that influences how your plants interact with each other and their environment. A thoughtful design takes into account the needs of pollinators, the efficient use of space, and the timing of planting and harvesting. Let's explore how to create a garden layout that maximizes the symbiotic relationships inherent in companion planting.

Planning for Pollinators

Pollinators are crucial to the success of many gardens, as they play a vital role in the reproduction of many plants. Designing your garden to attract and support pollinators can significantly enhance its productivity and health. Consider including a variety of flowering plants that bloom at different times throughout the growing season to provide a continuous food source for pollinators. For example, lavender and sage bloom early in the season, while sunflowers and echinacea take over in late summer. Additionally, the arrangement of these plants can impact their attractiveness to pollinators. Clustering flowering plants in groups rather than spacing them out can make them more visible and accessible to bees and butterflies. Also, including features such as shallow water baths or nectar-rich plants can create a welcoming habitat for these vital garden helpers. By considering the needs of pollinators in your garden layout, you not only enhance the ecological balance but also ensure a more bountiful harvest.

Maximizing Space with Companion Planting

Companion planting is particularly beneficial for making the most of limited garden space. By carefully selecting plant pairs that complement each other, you can increase the overall productivity of your garden. For instance, tall plants like corn can provide shade for more heat-sensitive plants like lettuce, which can be planted at their base. This not only optimizes the use of vertical space but also reduces the evaporation of moisture from the soil, which benefits both plants. Similarly, vining plants such as peas can be trained to climb up trellises, freeing up ground space for low-growing, shade-tolerant herbs such as parsley or cilantro. This strategic use of space not only increases the variety of plants you can grow but also encourages a healthier garden by enhancing air circulation and reducing the spread of diseases.

Rotation and Succession Planting

Crop rotation and succession planting are time-tested strategies that can significantly enhance the health and productivity of your garden. Rotation involves changing the location of plant types in your garden each year to prevent the build-up of pests and diseases and to manage soil fertility. For example, following a nitrogen-fixing legume like beans with a nitrogen-loving vegetable like spinach can help maintain soil health without chemical fertilizers. Succession planting refers to the practice of planting new crops as others are harvested, which ensures a continuous supply of produce. For instance, once garlic is harvested in midsummer, the space can be used for a fast-growing crop like bush beans. Both of these strategies require thoughtful planning in your garden layout to ensure that each plant's needs are met without compromising the overall design and productivity of the garden.

Mapping Your Garden

Creating a visual map of your garden can be an invaluable tool in planning and maintaining your companion planting layout. Start by drawing a scale outline of your garden space, including any existing structures or plants. Use this map to experiment with different plant arrangements, keeping in mind the needs for sunlight, water, and soil type that you've previously assessed. This map should also consider the growth habits and heights of various plants to ensure that every plant has access to its required resources. For crops that will be rotated or succession planted, make notes on the map about timing and subsequent plantings. This living document can serve as a guide throughout the gardening season, helping you keep track of what is planted where and making it easier to plan for future seasons.

As you finalize the design of your companion planting garden, remember that this layout serves as your roadmap to a lush, productive, and harmonious garden. The thoughtful placement of each plant, the consideration given to pollinators, and the strategic use of space all combine to create a dynamic garden ecosystem. By following the guidelines outlined in this chapter, you will be well-equipped to cultivate a garden that is not only a source of great joy and produce but also a vibrant example of ecological gardening practices. As we turn the page to the next chapter, we'll build on these foundational strategies, exploring the diverse world of plants that can enrich and enliven your garden through companion planting.

Chapter 3:
The Building Blocks

IMAGINE STEPPING INTO A LUSH, vibrant garden where every plant not only thrives but also contributes to the flourishing of its neighbors. This isn't just a dream; it's a practical reality that you can achieve in your own backyard through the strategic use of companion planting. At the heart of this approach are certain key players that act much like the foundations of a building, supporting and enhancing the overall structure. One of the most pivotal of these are the nitrogen fixers—remarkable plants that have the unique ability to pull nitrogen from the air and fix it into the soil in a form that other plants can absorb and use. This chapter delves into the world of nitrogen fixers and their crucial role in your garden, providing you with the knowledge to harness their benefits effectively.

3.1 Identifying Nitrogen Fixers and Their Garden Allies

The Role of Nitrogen Fixers

Nitrogen is a vital nutrient for plants, essential for the synthesis of proteins and other key molecules that facilitate healthy growth and development. However, while atmospheric nitrogen is abundant, most plants cannot use it in its gaseous form. This is where nitrogen-fixing plants come into play. These plants, often legumes like peas, beans, and clover, have a symbiotic relationship with specific bacteria called Rhizobia, which inhabit nodules in their roots and convert atmospheric nitrogen into nitrates, a form that plants can readily absorb. This process not only benefits the nitrogen-fixing plants themselves but also enriches the soil with essential nitrogen, supporting the growth of neighboring plants. Incorporating these natural fertilizers into your garden can significantly reduce your reliance on chemical fertilizers, promoting a more organic and sustainable approach to gardening.

Examples of Nitrogen-Fixing Plants

The variety of nitrogen-fixing plants available offers a wide array of choices for your garden. Common examples include:

- *Legumes (Beans, Peas, and Lentils):* These plants are powerhouses in the garden, not only for their ability to fix nitrogen in the soil but also for their bountiful harvest of tasty and nutritious fruits. Legumes are versatile and can thrive in a variety of settings, from spacious vegetable gardens to compact containers, making them an excellent choice for gardeners with limited space. Incorporating legumes into your garden not only enriches the soil but also provides you with a rich source of proteins and vitamins from their edible fruits.

- *Clovers (Red and White Clover):* Often underestimated, clovers are more than just ornamental plants or lucky charms. Both red and white varieties are vigorous nitrogen fixers that can significantly enhance the fertility of your soil. Utilizing clovers as cover crops is a smart strategy for organic gardeners seeking to improve soil health naturally. Their dense growth also suppresses weeds and protects the soil from erosion, making them a multi-functional addition to your garden ecosystem.

- *Alfalfa:* This deep-rooted wonder is renowned for its ability to penetrate compacted soil layers, improving soil structure and aeration. Alfalfa's roots not only reach deep into the earth to access untapped nutrients but also contribute significantly to nitrogen enrichment in the soil. Its vigorous growth and beneficial effects on soil make alfalfa an excellent choice for gardeners looking to rejuvenate and enhance the fertility of their garden beds over time.

- *Lupins:* Lupins are not only known for their striking spikes of colorful flowers that add a splash of beauty to any garden but also for their role as efficient nitrogen fixers. The aesthetic appeal of lupins, combined with their ability to improve soil fertility, makes them an ideal choice for gardeners who wish to enjoy both visual beauty and practical benefits. Planting lupins among your vegetable rows can increase biodiversity, attracting beneficial insects while naturally boosting the nutrient content of your garden soil.

Companion Plants for Nitrogen Fixers

Pairing nitrogen fixers with other plants can maximize the benefits of enhanced soil nitrogen. For example, planting beans near corn allows the corn to take advantage of the nitrogen fixed by the beans, promoting healthier growth and higher yields. Similarly, pairing clover with leafy vegetables such as spinach or lettuce can improve leaf production due to the increased availability of nitrogen in the soil. Understanding which plants benefit most from proximity to nitrogen-fixers can help you make informed decisions about planting arrangements, leading to a more productive garden.

Integrating Nitrogen Fixers into Your Garden

Incorporating nitrogen fixers into your garden design requires thoughtful planning. Consider the following strategies:

- *Rotation:* Include nitrogen-fixing plants in your crop rotation schedule. After a crop that depletes soil nutrients, such as corn, rotate in a nitrogen-fixing legume to replenish the soil.
- *Interplanting:* Plant nitrogen fixers alongside other crops. For instance, intersperse rows of peas with carrots or radishes to enhance overall soil fertility.
- *Cover Cropping:* Use nitrogen-fixing plants as cover crops in the off-season. Plants like clover or vetch can cover bare soil, reducing erosion and increasing nitrogen levels for the next planting season.

Interactive Element: Garden Planning Exercise

Here's an exercise to help you integrate nitrogen fixers effectively. Draw a simple layout of your garden, marking areas with different sunlight exposures and soil types. Identify spots that might benefit from nitrogen enrichment—perhaps where heavy feeders will be planted next season. Choose suitable nitrogen-fixing plants for these areas and plan their placement in your garden layout. This exercise will not only help you optimize the use of nitrogen fixers but also enhance your overall garden planning skills.

3.2 The Significance of Pollinator-Attracting Plants

In every thriving garden, pollinators play a pivotal role, buzzing from flower to flower, facilitating the reproduction that ensures fruits and vegetables can develop. Understanding this, drawing these beneficial insects into your garden through companion planting isn't just helpful; it's transformative. Pollinators such as bees, butterflies, and even some birds are not only a delight to watch, but they significantly boost your garden's productivity and health. These creatures transfer pollen as they move from one bloom to another, a necessary step for many plants to produce seeds and fruit. Without them, you'd see a stark decrease in your garden's yield and the variety of plants thriving in it.

But how exactly does one turn their garden into a haven for these crucial garden allies? It starts with choosing the right plants. Flowers like lavender, cosmos, and zinnias are famously attractive to bees for their nectar and pollen. However, it's not just about beauty; herbs like borage and oregano also pull double duty by enticing pollinators while providing your kitchen with fresh flavors. Similarly, sunflowers, with their large, nectar-rich heads, are excellent at drawing pollinators and also serve as a natural trellis for climbing plants like cucumbers or beans, showcasing the dual benefits of thoughtful plant selection. By integrating these into your garden, you not only create a buzzing eco-hub but also enhance the overall productivity and health of your plant community.

Creating a layout that maximizes pollination requires more than just planting a range of attractive flowers. It involves thoughtful consideration of plant location, flowering time, and the needs of the pollinators themselves. Designing your garden so that there are always plants in bloom throughout the growing season ensures that pollinators have a consistent source of food. This can be achieved by staggering plantings and choosing species that bloom at different times. For instance, early bloomers like crocus and hyacinth can kick off the season, followed by mid-season bloomers like bee balm and coneflower, and later, asters and goldenrod can provide late-season sustenance for bees preparing for winter. Additionally, grouping flowering plants together rather than spacing them out can make it easier for pollinators to locate and move among them, increasing the efficiency of their work and the likelihood of pollination. Consider also the heights of different plants, ensuring smaller plants aren't overshadowed by taller ones, so each has its moment in the sun, quite literally, to attract its pollinator.

Maintaining a pollinator-friendly garden is an ongoing process that extends beyond planting the right flowers and designing effectively. It involves practicing gardening habits that support the health and safety of pollinators. This includes avoiding the use of pesticides, which can be harmful or even lethal to these insects. Instead, opt for natural pest control methods or manually remove pests from plants. Providing a source of water, such as a shallow birdbath or a saucer filled with pebbles and water, can also help pollinators stay hydrated and encourage them to return to your garden regularly. Remember, the goal is to create an environment where pollinators can not only visit but thrive and continue their vital role in the ecosystem. By taking these steps, you ensure that your garden is more than just a collection of plants; it becomes a dynamic ecosystem that supports and sustains a wide array of life, contributing to the biodiversity of your local environment. This approach not only enriches your gardening experience but also plays a part in broader environmental conservation efforts, making each choice a statement of care for the natural world.

3.3 Utilizing Cover Crops for Soil Health

Cover crops, often the unsung heroes of the sustainable garden, play a pivotal role in maintaining and enhancing the fertility and structure of your soil. These are plants primarily grown not for harvest but for the benefits they provide to the soil and subsequent plantings. They can be grasses, legumes, or other green plants used to cover the soil in and out of the regular growing season. What makes cover crops so beneficial? They protect the soil from erosion, improve soil composition, and can even help manage weed and pest populations. This is especially useful in a companion planting setup where the health of one plant can influence its neighbors.

When choosing the right cover crops for your garden, it's crucial to consider your specific gardening needs and the main benefits each type of cover crop offers. For instance, leguminous cover crops such as vetch or clover can fix nitrogen in the soil, making it available for future crops that require nitrogen in large quantities. Non-leguminous crops, like rye or barley, are excellent for adding organic matter and improving soil structure. They also tend to grow quickly, providing a dense canopy that suppresses weeds and protects the soil from erosion. Each type of cover crop brings a unique set of benefits, so selecting the right ones can greatly enhance the specific needs of your garden soil and the plants that will follow.

The benefits of incorporating cover crops into your garden plan are numerous and impactful. Firstly, they play a significant role in erosion control. Their roots hold the soil in place, preventing it from being washed or blown away during harsh weather conditions. This is particularly important in raised beds or sloped gardens where soil erosion can be a significant problem. Secondly, as cover crops decompose, they add essential organic matter back into the soil. This organic matter improves soil fertility by increasing nutrient content and enhancing the soil's ability to retain water. Additionally, the decomposition process helps to aerate the soil and encourages the proliferation of beneficial microorganisms. Another significant benefit is weed suppression. Fast-growing cover crops like oats or buckwheat can outcompete weeds, which reduces the need for manual weeding and the use of chemical herbicides. These advantages make cover crops an invaluable component of an integrated garden management system, particularly in a companion planting framework where the overall health of the garden ecosystem is interconnected.

Integrating cover crops into your garden plan requires strategic thinking about when and where to plant them. In a companion planting system, you might consider planting cover crops during the off-season to prepare the soil for the next growing cycle. For example, after harvesting summer vegetables, planting a winter cover crop like crimson clover can help fix nitrogen in the soil and prepare it for nitrogen-hungry spring crops. In terms of placement, consider areas of your garden that might be left fallow during certain seasons or spots where soil compaction or erosion is a concern. These areas can particularly benefit from the protective and restorative properties of cover crops. Additionally, think about the lifecycle of your main crops and how cover crops can be rotated or interplanted to complement these cycles. For instance, after harvesting early vegetables, a quick-growing cover crop can be sown to cover the bare soil, suppressing weeds and preparing the soil with needed nutrients for the next planting.

Incorporating cover crops into your garden is not just about planting them at the right time and place. It's also about managing them correctly to maximize their benefits. This might involve mowing or trimming cover crops before they set seed to prevent them from becoming weed problems in the future. It also includes knowing when to turn them into the soil to optimize the decomposition process and nutrient release. Ideally, this should be done a few weeks before you plan to plant your next crop to allow enough time for the cover crops to decompose adequately. By managing cover crops effectively, you ensure that your garden soil remains healthy, fertile, and well-structured, supporting a diverse and productive companion planting system. Through this thoughtful integration and management, cover crops not only enhance the health of your garden soil but also contribute to the sustainability and productivity of your entire garden ecosystem.

3.4 Pest Deterrent Plants and How to Use Them

In the vibrant tapestry of your garden, every plant not only contributes beauty but can also serve a protective role, especially when it comes to managing pests naturally. This strategy, often overlooked, harnesses the inherent properties of certain plants to repel pests, reducing the need for chemical interventions. By understanding how these plants work and integrating them strategically into your garden, you can create a more harmonious environment that naturally minimizes pest issues.

Natural Pest Control

The concept of using plants for pest control is rooted in the natural defenses that plants have developed over millennia. Certain plants emit smells or chemicals that pests find offensive or confusing. These can be used to your advantage by planting them in or around your garden to naturally deter pests. For example, many pests are repelled by strong scents; thus, aromatic plants like lavender, rosemary, and peppermint can be powerful allies. These plants produce essential oils that many garden pests find undesirable. Additionally, the physical structure of some plants can act as a barrier or deterrent. For instance, the hairy leaves of borage are known to discourage many insects just by their texture.

Examples of Pest Deterrent Plants

Several plants are renowned for their pest-repelling qualities. Marigolds, with their bright blooms, are not just eye candy for your garden but are also effective at repelling nematodes and other pests when planted around vegetables like tomatoes and peppers. Garlic, though not typically thought of as a companion plant, can be interplanted with roses to ward off aphids. Chrysanthemums contain pyrethrins, a natural insecticide that is effective against many insects and can be planted throughout the garden to protect a variety of other plants. Including these plants in your garden not only adds diversity and beauty but also fortifies your garden's natural defense system against pests.

Strategic Placement for Maximum Effect

The placement of pest deterrent plants can significantly enhance their effectiveness. To utilize these plants most effectively, consider the specific pests you are targeting and the plants they are known to affect. For example, if your vegetable patch has been previously affected by root-knot nematodes, planting marigolds in that area can help reduce their numbers in the soil. For airborne pests like aphids, planting garlic around susceptible plants can help keep them at bay. The key is to integrate these pest deterrent plants directly within or around the perimeter of the areas where vulnerable plants are located, creating a natural barrier that protects while enhancing the overall health and aesthetic of your garden.

Complementary Pest Management Strategies

While using pest deterrent plants is an effective strategy, it is most effective when used as part of a broader integrated pest management approach. This might include practices like crop rotation, which minimizes pest buildup by changing the crops in a particular area each season. Companion planting can also play a role; for instance, planting onions near carrots can help repel carrot flies. Additionally, encouraging beneficial insects by providing habitats such as insect hotels or patches of nettles can enhance natural pest control. These insects, such as ladybugs, lacewings, and hoverflies, are natural predators of many common garden pests and can help keep their populations in check. By combining these strategies with the use of pest deterrent plants, you can create a comprehensive pest management plan that keeps your garden healthy and thriving naturally.

In this chapter, we explored how integrating certain plants into your garden can serve as a natural deterrent to pests. These plants, by virtue of their scents or physical makeup, offer a natural means to protect your garden, reducing the need for chemical pesticides. By strategically placing these plants and using additional complementary pest management strategies, you can maintain a healthy balance in your garden ecosystem. This approach not only ensures healthier plants but also contributes to a more sustainable gardening practice.

As we conclude this chapter, remember that each plant in your garden holds potential beyond its aesthetic or nutritional value; it can play a crucial role in the natural management of pests. Embracing this concept as part of your gardening strategy opens up new avenues for creating a garden that is not only productive and beautiful but also resilient and self-sustaining. As we move forward, we will continue to explore more ways in which you can enhance your garden's health and productivity through innovative and natural gardening practices.

Chapter 4:
The First Steps

STEPPING INTO THE REALM OF companion planting is like being introduced to a dance where each participant enhances the performance of the other. This chapter is your guide to selecting your first dance partners — the plants that will set the stage for a harmonious and productive garden. You might feel a bit like a choreographer, deciding who should pair with whom, but fear not! I'm here to lead you through these first exciting steps, ensuring that each plant you choose will help create a beautiful ensemble, rather than stepping on each other's toes.

4.1 Selecting Your First Companion Plants

When beginning your companion planting adventure, simplicity is your best friend. Starting with easy-to-grow plant pairs can boost your confidence and provide early successes that fuel your gardening passion. A classic and forgiving pairing for beginners is tomatoes and basil. Not only do these plants grow well together, but they also benefit each other. Basil is known to improve the flavor of tomatoes, and its strong scent can help deter pests that might otherwise target your tomato plants. Another excellent pairing for novices is carrots and onions. Onions can help repel the carrot fly, a common pest for carrots, by masking their scent with their own pungent aroma.

The benefits of companion planting go beyond just pest control. Understanding what each plant offers its neighbor is key to creating a thriving garden. For instance, consider the well-loved combination of beans, corn, and squash, often referred to as the "Three Sisters." In this trio, corn provides a natural trellis for beans to climb, beans fix nitrogen in the soil to the benefit of the nutrient-hungry corn and squash, and the broad leaves of squash help retain moisture in the soil, suppress weed growth, and provide a living mulch, thereby benefiting all three. Each plant in this group not only lives but thrives due to the support of its companions, illustrating the power of strategic plant partnerships.

However, even with the best intentions, mistakes can happen, especially when you're new to the world of gardening. A common pitfall in companion planting is overcrowding, where plants are placed too close together, leading to competition rather than cooperation. This can stress the plants and reduce their productivity. For example, while it might be tempting to pack as many herbs as possible around your tomatoes for their protective benefits, too little space can restrict air circulation, which increases the risk of fungal diseases. Always consider the mature size of each plant and provide enough space between them to grow fully.

Seasonal considerations are also crucial when selecting companion plants. Not all plants thrive in the same seasons, and understanding this can prevent unintentional mismatches. For instance, planting cool-season lettuces near warm-season peppers might work in the spring, but as the summer heats up, the lettuces can bolt (flower prematurely), which makes them bitter and less palatable. Instead, consider timing your plantings so that the lettuces will be harvested by the time the summer heat begins in earnest, or plant them on the north side of taller crops like tomatoes or corn to provide some natural shade and extend their growing season.

Interactive Element: Seasonal Planting Reflection

Take a moment to think about the seasonal climates in your area. Reflect on which plants might thrive best in each season and jot down a list. Consider how these plants could interact with each other. Could a summer crop benefit from the leftover nitrogen fixed by a spring crop of beans? Could a fall crop of leafy greens benefit from the shading provided by the remnants of a summer corn crop? This exercise will help you visualize and plan a garden that remains productive throughout multiple growing seasons, using the principles of companion planting to make the most of each plant's natural tendencies and strengths.

By choosing the right companion plants and understanding the intricacies of their interactions, you set the stage for a garden that is not only productive but also a joy to maintain. Remember, each plant in your garden plays a part in a larger community — think of yourself as the community organizer, bringing together the right plants to support, enhance, and celebrate each other's growth.

4.2 Creating a Planting Schedule: When and Where to Plant

In the world of gardening, timing isn't just a minor detail—it's a central element that can dictate the success or failure of your garden. Think of your garden as a stage where each plant must make its debut at just the right moment to contribute to the ongoing show, which lasts from spring through fall. Creating a planting schedule that aligns with the natural growth cycles and needs of your plants is crucial. It ensures that each plant gets the best possible start, leading to optimal growth and abundant yields. When planning your garden's planting schedule, consider the different growth rates and seasonal preferences of each plant. For instance, cool-season crops like spinach and peas thrive in the cooler days of early spring and fall and should be planted accordingly. On the other hand, warm-season crops such as tomatoes, peppers, and cucumbers prefer the heat of summer and won't fare well until the danger of frost has passed.

To really fine-tune your planting schedule, pay attention to the local frost dates and monitor the soil temperature, which can be more indicative of planting readiness than air temperature alone. Most seed packets and gardening guides provide information on the best soil temperatures for planting specific seeds. For example, while peas can germinate in soil as cool as 40 degrees Fahrenheit, tomatoes require a much cozier 60 degrees or warmer. This attention to temperature helps prevent premature planting, which can lead to poor germination, stunted growth, or even plant death due to unexpected late frosts. By waiting for just the right temperature window, you give your plants the best possible start.

In addition to timing your planting according to temperature and season, understanding the spatial requirements of your garden is equally important. Each plant has its own space needs that, if met, help prevent competition for light, water, and nutrients. Spacing your plants properly also ensures adequate air circulation, which is crucial in preventing the spread of fungal diseases. When planning where and how to plant, consider the mature size of each plant and space them out accordingly. This might mean spacing rows of corn at least 30 inches apart, while clusters of radishes might only require six inches between them. Similarly, planting depth is vital for proper root development. Each type of plant has an ideal depth that places the seeds or roots in a zone of the soil that provides optimal conditions for growth. For example, large seeds like those of beans and peas do well when planted about an inch deep, allowing for enough soil coverage to maintain moisture while not being so deep that the seedling struggles to surface.

Succession planting is a strategy that can significantly enhance the productivity of your garden by ensuring a continuous supply of produce. This technique involves planting new crops in intervals throughout the growing season rather than planting all at once. For example, instead of planting all your lettuce seeds at the same time, you could plant a new batch every two weeks. This method extends the harvest period, as mature plants can be harvested over a longer time rather than all at once. Succession planting can be particularly effective with fast-growing crops like greens and radishes, which can go from seed to harvest in just a few weeks. It requires careful scheduling and might mean preparing additional sections of your garden in advance, but the reward is a garden that keeps on giving right through the season.

By carefully considering the timing of your plantings, the specific needs of each plant, and employing techniques like succession planting, you can create a garden that is both bountiful and beautiful. This thoughtful approach to scheduling and plant placement helps ensure that every plant performs its best, contributing to a lush and productive garden. As you continue to plan and plant, remember that each choice you make builds on the last, creating a complex interplay of elements that all contribute to the garden's overall success.

4.3 Seed Starting and Transplanting Basics

Embarking on the adventure of growing your own plants from seeds can be one of the most rewarding experiences in gardening. It allows you to watch the miracle of life as tiny seeds transform into beautiful plants. However, successful seed starting requires understanding some fundamental techniques that can improve germination rates and ensure healthy seedlings. One effective method is pre-soaking seeds, especially those with hard shells like peas and beans. By soaking these seeds in room-temperature water overnight, you can soften their outer coatings, which encourages quicker and more uniform germination. Another crucial aspect is temperature control. Most seeds have specific temperature needs for optimal germination; for instance, tomatoes and peppers germinate best when soil temperatures are between 70-80°F. Using a heat mat under your seed trays can help maintain this ideal temperature, especially in cooler climates or during early spring when indoor temperatures might be lower.

After your seeds have sprouted, the next critical phase is transplanting young plants into the garden. This step can be daunting, as young seedlings are delicate and prone to shock if not handled carefully. To ensure a smooth transition, start by preparing the garden bed properly, making it free of weeds, and amending it with compost to provide a nutrient-rich environment for new plants. When removing seedlings from their trays or pots, be gentle to avoid damaging the roots. Make a hole in the prepared soil large enough to accommodate the entire root ball, and place the seedling in so that the base of the stem is level with the soil surface. Gently firm the soil around the roots and water immediately to help settle the soil and eliminate air pockets, which can dry out the roots. This careful handling helps seedlings to recover more rapidly from the transplant shock.

Hardening off seedlings is another vital step that gardeners must not overlook. This process involves gradually acclimating indoor-grown plants to outdoor conditions. Seedlings raised indoors are accustomed to stable temperatures and low light levels and can be shocked by direct sunlight and variable weather. To harden off seedlings, begin by placing them outside in a shaded, protected area for a few hours each day, gradually increasing their exposure to sun and wind over a week or two. This gradual introduction helps them to build resilience and reduces stress, leading to stronger, more adaptable plants. Always keep an eye on the weather during this period and be ready to bring plants indoors if late frosts threaten or if temperatures drop dramatically.

Choosing between direct sowing and transplanting seedlings can significantly affect the management and outcome of your garden. Each method has its benefits and considerations. Direct sowing involves planting seeds directly into your garden soil. This method is ideal for plants that are sensitive to root disturbance or that grow quickly, such as carrots and radishes. It eliminates the shock associated with transplanting and can lead to stronger, more resilient plants. However, it also means that seeds may be more susceptible to weather fluctuations, soil conditions, and pests. On the other hand, starting seeds indoors and transplanting seedlings allows for greater control over the growing environment, including temperature, moisture, and light. This can lead to healthier, more robust seedlings and an extended growing season, especially in regions with shorter summers. However, it requires more time and resources, and the risk of transplant shock can be higher if not managed correctly.

As you navigate these initial stages of garden setup, from starting seeds to placing young plants in your garden, remember that each step you take is building the foundation for a flourishing garden. By mastering these basics, you ensure that your plants get the best possible start, setting the stage for a season of growth and bounty.

4.4 Simple Watering and Fertilization Techniques for Companion Plants

Efficient watering practices form the cornerstone of a thriving garden, especially when nurturing a variety of companion plants. Each plant has unique moisture needs, and understanding how to meet these without wastage is crucial. Watering at the root zone is one effective technique that ensures water goes directly to where it's most needed—the roots—rather than splashing on the leaves, which can lead to fungal diseases or evaporation. Utilize soaker hoses or drip irrigation systems laid out near the base of the plants. These methods deliver water slowly and directly to the soil, minimizing runoff and evaporation, and providing a deep watering that encourages roots to grow downwards, fostering stronger and more resilient plants. This method is particularly beneficial in companion planting setups where plants of varying water needs coexist. For example, by placing the drip lines strategically, you can ensure that water-loving plants like celery receive ample moisture, while nearby drought-tolerant herbs like rosemary receive less.

Transitioning to natural fertilization methods, compost and manure tea are superb organic choices that not only feed the plants but also improve soil structure and encourage beneficial microbial activity. Compost, rich in nutrients, can be added to the soil at the time of planting or used as a top dressing during the growing season. It slowly releases nutrients into the soil, providing a steady food source. Manure tea, made by steeping well-aged manure in water, is another excellent organic fertilizer that can be applied directly to the soil around your plants or used as a foliar spray. This nutrient-rich concoction provides a quick boost of nitrogen, phosphorus, and potassium, which are essential for healthy plant growth. When using these natural fertilizers, it's vital to ensure they are well-composted or aged to avoid the introduction of pathogens to your garden and to prevent the burning of plants with too strong a concentration.

Monitoring plant health is key to successful gardening and becomes especially vital when you're managing the diverse needs of companion-planted gardens. Keep an eye out for signs of over or under-watering; wilting, yellowing leaves can often indicate that a plant is receiving too much or too little water. Similarly, signs of nutrient deficiencies must be addressed promptly. Yellow leaves can also indicate a nitrogen deficiency, purpling of the leaf may suggest a phosphorus deficit, and browning edges might reveal a lack of potassium. Regularly inspect your plants for these symptoms and adjust your watering and fertilization practices accordingly. Observing and responding to these cues promptly can help prevent more severe damage and keep your garden thriving.

Adapting your watering and fertilization practices according to the seasons is crucial for maintaining a healthy garden throughout the year. In the warmer months, evaporation rates are higher, and plants generally require more water. Conversely, during cooler months, plants' water needs decrease, and overwatering can lead to root rot or fungal diseases. The same seasonal adjustment applies to fertilization; plants benefit from a more robust feeding schedule during their peak growing season, usually in the spring and summer, when they are actively growing and producing. As the growing season winds down, reduce the frequency of fertilization to prevent the promotion of new growth that will be vulnerable to winter damage.

Wrapping Up: Fostering Growth with Water and Nutrients

In this chapter, we explored the essentials of watering and fertilizing your companion plants, focusing on efficiency and sustainability. By adopting methods like targeted watering at the root zone and using organic fertilizers such as compost and manure tea, you not only cater to each plant's unique needs but also contribute to a more sustainable gardening practice. Monitoring your plants regularly for any signs of distress and adjusting your care routine in response to seasonal changes ensures your garden remains vigorous and productive throughout the year.

As we move forward, remember that these foundational practices set the stage for a flourishing garden, where the harmony between plants is matched by your attuned care strategies. Next, we'll explore how to protect this carefully cultivated harmony by naturally managing pests and diseases, ensuring your garden remains a resilient and bountiful haven.

Chapter 5:
Advanced Strategies

IMAGINE YOUR GARDEN AS A dynamic stage where each season brings a new act, a fresh set of characters, and evolving interactions that enrich your plot. As you become more versed in the basic rhythms of companion planting, you might find yourself curious about more sophisticated strategies that can further enhance your garden's performance. In this chapter, we dive into the art of crop rotation—a practice as ancient as agriculture itself, yet remarkably effective in modern companion planting. This method not only invigorates your garden but also introduces a rhythm to your planting strategy that aligns with the natural cycles of the earth and the seasons.

5.1 Crop Rotation and Its Benefits in Companion Planting

Breaking Pest and Disease Cycles

One of the most compelling reasons to implement crop rotation in your garden is its ability to disrupt the life cycles of pests and diseases naturally. Many pests and plant diseases thrive under continuous conditions where their preferred hosts are always available. By rotating crops—changing what's planted where each season—you essentially pull the rug out from under these unwelcome guests. For instance, if tomatoes were plagued by a specific soil-borne fungus one year, planting them in the same spot the next year would likely invite a recurrence. However, replacing them with a non-susceptible crop like beans or garlic can break the disease cycle, reducing the risk of infection. Similarly, crop rotation can confuse pests that return to previous feeding grounds only to find that their preferred food source is no longer there. This simple yet strategic move can keep your garden healthier and reduce your reliance on chemical interventions.

Nutrient Management

Crop rotation also plays a crucial role in managing soil nutrients and preventing depletion. Different plants have varying nutrient needs; for example, leafy greens may deplete nitrogen levels in the soil, while legumes naturally add nitrogen back into it. By rotating a nitrogen-consuming crop like corn with a nitrogen-fixing crop like peas, you can help maintain balanced soil fertility without external inputs. This not only keeps the soil healthy but also ensures that each plant has access to the nutrients it needs to thrive. Over time, this practice can lead to richer soil and more bountiful harvests, as each crop contributes something to the soil before the next takes its place.

Planning Your Rotation

Implementing an effective crop rotation plan requires some forethought and organization. Start by dividing your crops into categories based on their family and nutrient needs—for instance, nightshades (tomatoes, peppers), legumes (beans, peas), and brassicas (cabbage, kale). Aim to rotate crops from different categories into each garden plot over several seasons. A simple rotation might look something like this: Year 1—Tomatoes, Year 2—Beans, Year 3—Kale. This sequence helps prevent the overlap of pests and diseases common to each family and balances nutrient demands. To keep track of your rotation schedule, maintain a garden journal or map where you record what's planted where each year, making it easier to plan future rotations.

Examples of Effective Crop Rotations

To give you a clearer picture, consider these tailored rotation plans for different garden sizes and types:

- *Small Vegetable Garden:* Begin with tomatoes in plot one, squash in plot two, and lettuce in plot three. The following year, rotate each crop to the next plot. Continue this rotation to balance soil nutrients and pest management.
- *Herb and Vegetable Garden:* Plant basil and tomatoes together in one section, carrots and onions in another, and beans and cucumbers in a third. Next season, rotate each group to a new section to deter pests and optimize soil conditions.

Interactive Element: Rotation Planning Exercise

Here's a straightforward exercise to kick-start your crop rotation plan. Draw a rough outline of your garden, and divide it into three or more sections, depending on the number of different crops you grow. Assign each section a crop category as mentioned above. Now, using colored pencils or markers, rotate these categories through the sections in your drawing for the next three years. This visual aid will not only help you understand the rotation concept but also serve as a practical guide when planting season arrives.

Incorporating crop rotation into your companion planting strategy is like choreographing a dance where each step enriches the performer and enhances the performance. This ancient practice, refreshed and applied in modern gardening, promises a garden that remains vibrant, productive, and healthy, season after season. As you adopt these advanced strategies, your role evolves from a gardener to an eco-strategist, orchestrating the interplay of nature's own cycles with human ingenuity to create a sustainable, flourishing garden.

5.2 Succession Planting to Maximize Garden Yield

Imagine your garden offering a continuous bounty, where something is always ready to harvest, from the first tender leaves of spring to the last hearty root vegetables of fall. This dream can become your garden's reality with the strategic use of succession planting. Succession planting is a method where you stagger the planting of crops to extend the harvesting period, ensuring a steady supply of fresh produce throughout the growing season. This technique is particularly effective in companion planting setups, where the thoughtful combination of different plants can optimize the use of space and resources, enhancing overall garden productivity.

The concept of an extended harvest window is simple yet transformative. Typically, a vegetable garden planted all at once will have a peak harvest time, after which the garden may look bare until the next planting season. By planning successive plantings, you can have waves of production rather than a single harvest. For example, instead of planting all your lettuce seeds at once, you could plant a portion of them every two weeks. This method ensures that as one batch of lettuce is being harvested, another is just coming into maturity, providing you with a continuous supply of fresh greens. Similarly, by planting fast-maturing crops like radishes or spinach in between rows of slower-growing vegetables like broccoli or tomatoes, you can harvest the quick crops before the others need more room to expand, maximizing your garden's output without wasting space.

Implementing strategies for succession planting involves more than just timing; it requires a thoughtful approach to the selection and combination of plants. Intercropping, where you grow one crop alongside or between another, is a practical method in succession planting. This can be as simple as planting quick-growing herbs or leafy greens in the spaces between slower-maturing plants like peppers or eggplants. The key is to choose companion plants that do not compete aggressively for the same resources. Another effective method is relay planting, where you start a new crop in the same space as another crop that is nearing the end of its productive period. For instance, as your early crop of peas begins to fade, you can plant a crop of beans that will mature later in the season. These methods not only ensure continuous productivity but also help maintain soil health and reduce weed pressure, as there are fewer open areas in the garden.

When planning your garden with succession planting in mind, it's crucial to select companion plants that support each other's growth cycles. Consider the differing nutrient needs and growth habits of your plants. For example, after harvesting a nitrogen-heavy feeder like corn, you might plant nitrogen-fixing legumes in the same area to replenish the soil. Similarly, following a deep-rooted vegetable like carrots with a shallow-rooted crop such as lettuce can help make full use of the soil's nutrients and space. This thoughtful selection and timing of companion plants not only optimize your garden's productivity but also enhance the health and balance of your garden ecosystem.

Case Studies: Real-Life Succession Planting

To illustrate the effectiveness of succession planting in a companion garden, let's look at a couple of real-life examples. In one urban community garden, gardeners implemented a rotation of leafy greens and root vegetables throughout the season. They started with spinach and radishes in early spring, followed by lettuces and turnips. Mid-season, they planted kale and beets, and late in the season, they sowed collards and carrots. This rotation provided the community with a variety of vegetables throughout the year and improved soil health by varying the type and depth of root systems in the garden beds.

In another case, a home gardener used a combination of vertical and succession planting to maximize her small space. She planted climbing peas early in the season on a trellis, with lettuce underneath to take advantage of the shade provided by the maturing pea plants. As the peas were harvested, she planted cucumber seeds at the base of the same trellis, which then used the now-vacant structure for support as they grew through the summer. This approach not only saved space but also kept the garden producing continuously throughout the growing season.

These examples showcase how succession planting can transform the productivity and sustainability of gardens of all sizes and types. By extending the harvest window, utilizing strategic planting strategies, and choosing compatible companion plants, you can create a garden that is not only a source of continual bounty but also a dynamic, living ecosystem that supports itself throughout the seasons. Whether you are a novice gardener or looking to refine your skills, incorporating succession planting into your gardening strategy opens up a world of possibilities for enhancing both the yield and enjoyment of your garden.

5.3 Utilizing Vertical Space in Companion Planting

When you start to think about your garden not just in terms of square footage but also in terms of cubic footage, a whole new world of possibilities opens up. This is the essence of vertical gardening—a smart, space-saving strategy that lets you grow more in less space while also enhancing the overall health and productivity of your garden. Vertical gardening is particularly advantageous in companion planting, where the strategic placement of plants can significantly influence their health and yield. By growing upwards instead of outwards, you not only maximize your planting area but also introduce a variety of other benefits that can transform your garden.

One of the primary advantages of vertical gardening is its ability to increase yield. When plants are arranged vertically, they can be spaced more closely, which means you can fit more plants into the same footprint. For example, vining plants like cucumbers, peas, and pole beans, which might sprawl across a large area if grown horizontally, can be trained to climb up a trellis, dramatically reducing their ground space requirements. This not only increases the number of plants you can grow but also makes each plant more accessible for maintenance and harvesting. Furthermore, vertical growth encourages plants to grow stronger and healthier. Vines that climb towards the sun expose more of their foliage to light, enhancing photosynthesis and potentially leading to better fruit production and healthier plants overall.

Another significant benefit of growing plants vertically is the reduction in pest and disease issues. When plants are elevated off the ground, they are less likely to come into contact with soil-borne pathogens and pests that could damage them. Air circulation around the plants also improves when they are grown vertically, which helps keep the foliage dry and less susceptible to fungal diseases. For instance, tomato plants, when trained to grow up a vertical support, often have fewer issues with fungal diseases like blight, which thrive in damp, poorly ventilated environments. Additionally, vertical structures can act as barriers to pests, providing physical protection to the plants and making it more difficult for pests like snails and certain insects to reach the plants.

Support Structures for Vertical Gardening

To successfully implement vertical gardening in your companion planting scheme, choosing the right support structures is crucial. These structures not only support the growth of climbing plants but also integrate seamlessly into the aesthetic of your garden. Trellises are one of the most common support structures and can be made from a variety of materials, including wood, metal, or even sturdy plastic. They are ideal for supporting a wide range of climbing plants, from beans and peas to flowering vines like morning glories or clematis, adding both functionality and beauty to your garden. Another popular option is garden towers, which are particularly useful for small spaces. These towers allow plants to grow upwards in a spiral pattern, maximizing the vertical space and making efficient use of the garden's footprint. Wall planters are another innovative solution, especially for gardeners who may not have traditional garden space. These can be attached to any vertical surface, such as a fence or wall, and can be used to grow a variety of herbs, small vegetables, and flowers, making every vertical surface a potential growing area.

Selecting Plants for Vertical Companion Planting

Choosing the right plants for vertical structures involves considering their climbing habits and compatibility with other plants. Some plants, like ivy or climbing roses, have natural tendrils that cling to surfaces, making them excellent choices for trellises or wire supports. Others, like cucumbers or squash, may need a little help and can be tied gently to supports as they grow. When selecting plants for vertical companion planting, consider their light, water, and nutrient needs to ensure compatibility. For instance, pairing a water-heavy plant like cucumber with a drought-tolerant plant may not be ideal unless you can provide localized watering solutions that meet each plant's needs without compromise.

Maintenance Tips for Vertical Gardens

Maintaining a vertical garden involves regular checks and care to ensure that plants remain healthy and well-supported. Regular pruning is crucial to manage growth and ensure that plants do not become too heavy for their supports. This not only keeps your garden looking tidy but also helps improve air circulation around the plants, reducing the risk of disease. Watering vertically grown plants can sometimes be challenging, as gravity tends to pull water away from the roots quickly. Using a drip irrigation system that delivers water directly to the roots can solve this problem, ensuring that plants receive the moisture they need without wastage. Additionally, because vertical gardens can dry out faster than traditional gardens, checking soil moisture levels frequently and adjusting your watering schedule accordingly is essential to keep your plants thriving.

By embracing vertical gardening within your companion planting strategy, you not only enhance the aesthetic appeal of your garden but also its functionality and productivity. This approach allows you to explore new dimensions in gardening, turning every vertical space into a potential lush, green canvas that supports a diverse range of plants. Whether you are working with a small balcony or a large backyard, vertical gardening offers a dynamic solution to space limitations, inviting you to look up and see the possibilities.

5.4 Companion Planting in Containers and Small Spaces

Embarking on a gardening adventure doesn't require vast expanses of land; even the smallest balcony or patio can become a lush, productive oasis with the right approach. Container gardening is a fantastic solution for garden enthusiasts who have more ambition than space. This method allows you to cultivate a wide array of plants, from herbs and flowers to vegetables and fruits, right at your doorstep. The key to successful container gardening lies in understanding the fundamentals, from selecting the right containers and soil to choosing plants that can thrive together even in confined spaces.

Container gardening begins with choosing the right type of container for your plants. The options are vast—traditional pots, modern fabric grow bags, repurposed barrels, or even recycled items like old buckets can serve as excellent plant homes. However, the material of the container can affect the soil's moisture retention and temperature. For instance, clay pots are porous and allow soil to breathe, reducing the risk of waterlogged roots. On the other hand, plastic containers retain moisture better and are lighter, but they can heat up quickly in direct sunlight, which might stress the plants. Each container type has its advantages and considerations, so selecting based on your plant's needs and your climate is crucial. Additionally, ensure that every container has adequate drainage holes to prevent excess water from accumulating, which could cause root rot.

The choice of soil is equally important in container gardening. Unlike garden beds, where soil amendments can gradually improve soil structure and fertility, containers require a high-quality potting mix from the start. This mix should be loose, well-draining, yet capable of retaining enough moisture to keep roots hydrated. Look for mixes that include components like peat moss, perlite, and compost, which provide a balanced environment for plant roots. You can also consider specialized mixes tailored for specific types of plants, such as succulents or acid-loving plants, to further optimize growth conditions.

Selecting the right companion plants for container gardening involves understanding which plants can coexist harmoniously in a limited space. Some plants, like tomatoes, are heavy feeders and prefer to live solo in their containers, while others, like herbs and leafy greens, have less demanding root systems and can share space more easily. For example, basil and chives can be planted together in a larger container, where both can benefit from regular harvesting to spur further growth. Another effective pairing could be strawberries and thyme; the thyme acts as a ground cover to reduce moisture loss, and its presence can deter pests that might target strawberry plants. When choosing companions, consider their water, nutrient, and space needs to ensure they can thrive together without competition.

Maximizing space in small garden areas often requires creativity and flexibility. Utilizing tiered plant stands or installing shelves on sunny walls can increase your growing area vertically, similar to how you might use trellises in a larger garden. Hanging baskets are another excellent way to grow plants like herbs, strawberries, or trailing flowers, making use of overhead space that would otherwise go unused. These solutions not only expand your planting options but also add depth and visual interest to your garden, transforming it into a multi-dimensional living landscape.

Watering and fertilization in container gardens require a mindful approach, as the confined soil can dry out faster than in-ground beds and is solely reliant on you for nutrients. Watering needs can vary significantly between plants, but as a general rule, container plants require more frequent watering than those in the ground. Check the soil moisture daily, and consider self-watering containers or drip irrigation systems for consistent moisture, especially if you travel frequently or have a large number of containers. Fertilization should be regular but balanced; over-fertilizing can lead to nutrient burn, while under-fertilizing can starve your plants. Use a diluted liquid fertilizer every two weeks or a slow-release granular fertilizer at the beginning of the season to keep your plants well-fed and healthy.

By embracing container gardening and the principles of companion planting, you can create a vibrant, productive garden in any small space. This approach not only maximizes your available area but also enhances the health and yield of your plants, bringing the joys of gardening into more compact and controlled environments. As you adapt these strategies to your own space, you'll discover the endless possibilities that container gardening offers, proving that size is not a constraint but an opportunity for creativity.

As this chapter closes, reflect on how even the smallest spaces can yield abundant harvests and vibrant beauty when approached with knowledge and creativity. Each container is a microcosm of the larger garden ecosystem, capable of supporting life and providing sustenance. As we transition into the next chapter, we will explore how to protect and nurture these compact ecosystems through natural pest and disease management, ensuring your garden remains a resilient oasis no matter its size.

Chapter 6:
Your Companion Planting List

IMAGINE STEPPING INTO YOUR GARDEN, where each plant not only thrives in its own space but also contributes to the vitality of its neighbors. This harmonious interaction isn't just chance—it's the result of thoughtful companion planting. In this chapter, we delve into the heart of companion planting with a comprehensive guide designed to help you make informed decisions about which vegetables to plant together for the most beneficial relationships. Here, you'll find detailed pairings, understand the mutual benefits, and gain insights into optimal planting and spacing. This guide is more than a list; it's a tool to transform your garden into a thriving, interconnected ecosystem.

6.1 At-a-Glance List of Companion Plantings

I would say this is likely to be your most commonly referenced page, one that will become worn and tired—which is exactly what I'd love for you. Come back to this list often, and you'll learn what companions get on well (and which should be avoided as if they were enemies).

Plant	Good Companions	Avoid
Asparagus	Basil, Parsley, Tomatoes, Marigolds	Garlic, Onions, Potatoes
Basil	Tomatoes, Peppers, Oregano, Asparagus, Marigolds	Cucumbers
Beans	Carrots, Celery, Corn, Cucumbers, Eggplants, Peas, Potatoes, Radishes, Squash, Strawberries, Tomatoes	Fennel, Garlic, Onions
Beets	Onions, Garlic, Lettuce, Cabbage, Radishes, Mint	Field Mustard, Pole Beans
Broccoli	Beans, Carrots, Dill, Garlic, Onions, Radishes, Rosemary, Sage, Spinach	Peppers, Strawberries, Tomatoes
Cabbage	Beans, Chives, Leeks, Nasturtiums, Onions	Grapes, Peppers, Strawberries, Tomatoes
Carrots	Beans, Broccoli, Chives, Leeks, Lettuce, Onions, Peas, Radishes, Rosemary, Sage, Tomatoes	Celery, Dill, Parsnips
Chives	Carrots, Tomatoes, Grapes, Roses	Beans, Peas
Corn	Beans, Cucumbers, Peas, Squash	Celery, Eggplants, Tomatoes

Cucumbers	Beans, Corn, Dill, Lettuce, Oregano, Peas, Radishes, Sunflowers	Melons, Potatoes, Sage
Dill	Cabbage, Cucumbers, Lettuce, Onions, Basil	Carrots, Peppers
Eggplants	Basil, Spinach, Tomatoes	Fennel, Potatoes
Garlic	Carrots, Tomatoes, Lettuce, Beets, Spinach, Strawberries	Beans, Peas
Lettuce	Carrots, Radishes, Cucumbers, Strawberries, Onions	Celery, Parsley
Marigolds	Tomatoes, Peppers, Beans, Potatoes, Cucumbers	None significant, generally beneficial
Onions	Carrots, Lettuce, Strawberries, Beets, Tomatoes	Beans, Peas
Parsley	Tomatoes, Asparagus, Carrots, Corn	Mint
Peas	Basil, Beans, Carrots, Celery, Corn, Cucumbers, Lettuce, Radishes, Spinach, Tomatoes	Garlic, Onions, Potatoes
Peppers	Basil, Coriander, Onions, Spinach, Squash, Tomatoes	Beans, Brassicas (Broccoli, Cabbage), Fennel
Potatoes	Beans, Corn, Pumpkin	Cucumbers, Eggplants, Sunflowers, Tomatoes

Pumpkin	Corn, Beans, Marigolds	Potatoes
Radishes	Beans, Broccoli, Cabbage, Cucumbers, Lettuce, Peas, Tomatoes	Hyssop
Rosemary	Beans, Cabbage, Carrots, Sage	Cucumbers
Spinach	Beans, Carrots, Celery, Radishes, Strawberries	Fennel, Potatoes
Squash	Corn, Dill, Radishes, Sunflowers	Potatoes
Sunflowers	Corn, Cucumbers, Squash, Tomatoes	Potatoes
Thyme	Cabbage, Strawberries, Tomatoes	Cucumbers
Tomatoes	Asparagus, Basil, Beans, Carrots, Celery, Dill, Lettuce, Onions, Parsley, Radishes, Spinach, Thyme	Cabbage, Corn, Fennel, Potatoes

Notably, this list has been created for you as a beginners' reference, so while it isn't exhaustive, it certainly will be enough to get you started and headed in the right direction.

A Few Notes...

Just to help with expanding your gardening and companion planting knowledge a little more, here are some additional notes I'd like to share about the plants detailed in the table (not only because I'm a hopeless over-giver, but because, if you're anything like me, I find it all so fascinating...)

Asparagus: This is a long-lived perennial that benefits from being planted with tomatoes and basil, which are known to be particularly helpful with repelling asparagus beetles.

Basil: Not just a culinary herb, but a great companion for tomatoes and peppers owing to its recognized ability to repel pests and improve flavor.

Beets: Known to benefit from the companionship of onions and garlic, which can help to deter those crop-destroying pests.

Beans: Beans are nitrogen-fixers, enriching the soil for heavy feeders like corn and tomatoes, and make great companions by enhancing soil fertility.

Broccoli: Broccoli benefits from aromatic herbs like dill and rosemary, which repel pests like cabbage worms, making it a robust companion for other Brassicas.

Cabbage: Cabbage thrives when planted with onions and chives, which deter cabbage moths, while nasturtiums attract aphids away from the cabbage.

Carrots: Carrots pair well with onions and leeks, which repel carrot flies, and benefit from nitrogen-fixing plants like peas, making them great companions.

Chives: Helps deter aphids (the bane of a gardener's life), and can even enhance the flavor of tomatoes and carrots when planted nearby.

Corn: Corn is a key player in the "Three Sisters" planting method, supporting beans and squash, while benefiting from their nitrogen and weed suppression.

Cucumbers: Cucumbers benefit from dill, which attracts beneficial insects, and grow well with corn, which provides structural support and shade, so that our cucumbers can be cool and bring that refreshing flavor.

Dill: Attracts beneficial insects, but can inhibit the growth of carrots.

Eggplants: Eggplants thrive when planted alongside basil, which is known to be incredibly useful at repelling pests and enhancing flavor, making it the epitome of a beneficial companion.

Garlic: A powerful pest deterrent, particularly when used in the fight against aphids, though it notably can stunt the growth of legumes.

Lettuce: A versatile companion, it benefits from a variety of partners but can struggle near parsley.

Marigolds: Known for their pest-deterring properties, they're beneficial companions to most plants, so a must-have in any garden.

Onions: Good at deterring pests, though known to restrict the growth of legumes.

Parsley: Enhances the growth of tomatoes and asparagus, though can be invasive, in much the same way as mint.

Peas: Peas are known to be nitrogen-fixers that benefit heavy feeders like corn and work well with carrots and radishes, offering complementary growth habits.

Peppers: Peppers love the company of basil and marigolds, which repel pests and improve plant health, making them ideal companions in the vegetable garden.

Potatoes: Potatoes grow well with beans and corn, which help deter pests; however, they need to be kept away from tomatoes to avoid blight.

Pumpkin: Companionable with corn and beans, as per the "Three Sisters" planting tradition.

Radishes: Radishes deter pests like cucumber beetles when planted near cucumbers, and make great companions for lettuce and carrots.

Rosemary: A natural insect deterrent, especially when it comes to carrots and cabbages.

Spinach: Benefits from legumes that enrich the soil, though known to struggle near potatoes.

Squash: Squash benefits from the "Three Sisters" method when planted in the company of corn and beans, while marigolds help to deter those pesky squash bugs and other pests.

Sunflowers: Another must-have, known to attract beneficial insects, though should be avoided near potatoes due to their propensity to inhibit their growth.

Thyme: A natural pest deterrent, particularly for cabbage and strawberries.

Tomatoes: The perfect companion for basil, which improves flavor and repels pests, and marigolds, which help deter nematodes and aphids.

Notes on Avoided Companions:

- *Garlic and Onions:* These are often avoided with beans and peas as they can inhibit their growth.
- *Fennel:* Fennel has a tendency to inhibit the growth of many plants, which is why it appears frequently in the 'Avoid' column.
- *Potatoes:* Avoid planting potatoes near tomatoes, cucumbers, and squash due to the risk of blight and other diseases.
- *Tomatoes:* Avoid planting with corn and potatoes due to competition for nutrients and disease risks.

Furthermore, heavy feeders, such as broccoli, cabbage and cauliflower, should be avoided as companions to other heavy feeders, or no crop will grow to its maximum potential.

Moreover, be sure to consider those plants that will compete for space and nutrients, such as cucumbers and peppers.

And don't forget to be extremely careful when it comes to planting more invasive plants, like mint.

Jeff Tucker's

The Ultimate Handbook to Companion Planting for Beginners

Review Request Page

Make a Difference with Your Review
Subtitle: Unlock the Power of Generosity

"The greatest gift you can give your garden is the time and care to help it flourish." – Unknown

People who give without expecting anything in return often find the most joy. So, let's make a difference together!

Would you help someone just like you—eager to start companion planting but unsure where to begin?

My mission with The Ultimate Handbook to Companion Planting for Beginners is to make gardening easy and fun for everyone.

But to reach more curious gardeners, I need your help.

Most people choose books based on reviews. So, I'm asking you to help a fellow gardener by leaving a review.

It costs nothing and takes less than a minute, but your review could change someone's gardening journey. Your review could help...

...one more beginner grow a successful vegetable garden.
...one more family enjoy fresh, homegrown herbs.
...one more community create a shared garden space.
...one more backyard transform into a thriving ecosystem.
...one more dream of a greener world come true.

To make a difference, simply scan the QR code below and leave a review, or alternatively head to the following link:

https://www.amazon.com/review/review-your-purchases/?asin=B0DGM4NYBT

If you love helping others grow, you're my kind of person.

Thank you from the bottom of my heart!

—JEFF TUCKER

Vegetable Pairing Guidelines

The cornerstone of successful companion planting is knowing which vegetables grow well together and which combinations should be avoided. Some vegetables, like carrots and tomatoes, form a classic pairing, mutually enhancing each other's growth. Carrots are reputed to improve tomato plant health and flavor, while tomatoes, in return, repel carrot flies, protecting the roots of the carrots. On the other hand, pairing beans and onions can be detrimental; onions can inhibit the growth of beans by stunting their growth. Understanding these dynamics is crucial for planning a garden where each plant not only survives but thrives.

Benefits of Each Pairing

Each vegetable pairing in your garden can offer unique benefits. For instance, planting spinach and strawberries together helps to maximize your use of space and resources. Spinach provides ground cover, reducing weed growth and maintaining soil moisture, which benefits the strawberry plants. In return, the strawberries' sprawling habit can help protect spinach leaves from the harsh sun, keeping them tender and lush. These relationships can significantly improve plant health, yield, and flavor. By selecting companion plants that offer mutual benefits, you not only optimize your garden's productivity but also enhance its ecological balance.

Planting and Spacing Recommendations

Effective companion planting also involves strategic considerations about planting depth and spacing, which can vary significantly between different vegetable pairings. For example, when planting the aforementioned carrots and tomatoes together, it's advisable to sow carrot seeds about 3 to 4 inches away from tomato plants. This spacing allows carrots enough room to grow their roots while not encroaching on the tomato roots. Additionally, consider the planting sequence: sow carrot seeds a few weeks before planting tomato seedlings, giving carrots a head start. This staggered planting helps manage competition for nutrients and ensures both vegetables can establish themselves adequately in their shared space.

Troubleshooting Common Issues

Even with the best planning, you might encounter issues in your companion plantings. For instance, if your peas and cucumbers, which are generally good companions due to their similar structural needs for climbing support, start to exhibit signs of nutrient competition or inadequate growth, it may be necessary to reassess their placement or the timing of planting. Peas, being a cooler season crop, might benefit from an earlier planting than cucumbers, ensuring they don't compete too directly for sunlight and nutrients. Understanding and responding to such nuances can make a significant difference in the success of your companion planting efforts.

Interactive Element: Plant Pairing Exercise

To put this knowledge into practice, here's a simple exercise: Take a piece of paper and draw two columns. In the left column, list all the vegetables you wish to plant in your garden. In the right column, based on the guidelines provided, jot down potential companion plants for each vegetable. Consider factors like the benefits of each pairing and spacing recommendations. This visual pairing chart will serve as a practical reference when you are planning and implementing your garden layout. This exercise not only aids in visualizing your garden's potential but also ensures that each plant's needs are considered and met, paving the way for a lush, productive garden.

As you utilize this chapter to guide your vegetable planting decisions, remember that each plant in your garden can play a dual role—beautifying your space and enhancing the growth and health of its plant neighbors. The information here empowers you to make choices that lead to a more productive, beautiful, and harmonious garden. So, let's continue fostering these beneficial plant relationships and watch as your garden transforms into a vibrant tapestry of interconnected life.

6.2 Fruit Companion Planting

Fruit trees and berry bushes not only add beauty and shade to your garden but also provide delicious, fresh produce. To enhance the health and productivity of these valuable plants, incorporating companion planting is a smart strategy. Various companion plants can benefit fruit trees and berry bushes by improving soil health, enhancing pollination, and controlling pests naturally. For instance, consider planting chives around the base of apple trees. Chives help to deter pests like apple scab and can enhance the flavor and health of the apples. Similarly, planting legumes like clover in the orchard can increase nitrogen levels in the soil, which is beneficial for young fruit trees that require nitrogen to grow robustly.

Each type of fruit tree can benefit from specific companions. Peach trees, for example, thrive when planted near garlic, which helps repel borers and other pests that could damage the trees. Garlic has the added benefit of improving the flavor of the peaches. For citrus trees, consider planting marigolds around them; marigolds emit a scent that repels common pests like nematodes, which can harm the roots of citrus trees. Additionally, the bright flowers attract pollinators, aiding in the pollination of your fruit trees, which is essential for fruit production. These strategic plantings not only support the health and yield of your fruit trees but also add biodiversity and beauty to your garden landscape.

Berry bushes also greatly benefit from companion planting. Strawberries, for instance, pair well with borage. Borage strengthens strawberry plants and improves their flavor, and its blue flowers attract bees and other pollinators, which are crucial for strawberry pollination. Raspberries and blackberries can benefit from being planted near tansy or rue, which repel many of the common pests that afflict berry bushes. These companions help ensure that your berries remain healthy and abundant without the need for chemical pesticides. By understanding and implementing these beneficial pairings, you can create a more productive and sustainable berry patch in your garden.

Caring for the companion plants in your fruit garden is just as important as caring for the fruit plants themselves. Most companion plants require regular watering, although the amount and frequency can vary depending on the plant species and the local climate. For example, marigolds are relatively drought-tolerant and may need less water than more moisture-loving plants like borage. Pruning is also necessary for some companion plants to prevent them from overshadowing the fruit plants or competing with them for light and space. Regular harvesting of herbs and removal of spent blooms can encourage more vigorous growth and prevent the plants from taking over areas meant for your fruit trees and bushes.

Maximizing the yield and health of your fruit-bearing plants through companion planting involves more than just choosing the right partners; it requires a holistic approach to garden management. Ensuring that your fruit trees and berry bushes receive adequate sunlight, water, and nutrients, and are protected from pests and diseases, are all crucial components of a successful companion planting strategy. For example, ensuring that your fruit garden is well-mulched can help retain moisture in the soil, suppress weeds, and provide a slow-release source of nutrients to your plants. Additionally, implementing a rotational planting scheme where you plant different types of companions in different years can help prevent soil depletion and reduce pest and disease buildup.

By taking these steps, you enhance the immediate environment of your fruit trees and berry bushes and contribute to the overall health and productivity of your garden. This thoughtful approach to companion planting ensures that each plant not only survives but thrives, leading to a lush, vibrant, and fruitful garden.

6.3 Beneficial Herb Pairings and Their Uses

Herbs are not just culinary delights; they also play a pivotal role in the ecosystem of your garden. Integrating herbs among your vegetables and fruits can lead to a healthier, more aromatic, and visually appealing garden space. Herbs like basil, mint, and rosemary, when planted alongside other garden plants, offer a multitude of benefits, including natural pest deterrence and flavor enhancement for their neighboring plants. For instance, basil is well-known for its ability to repel flies and mosquitoes, making it a perfect companion for outdoor seating areas or alongside crops that are susceptible to these pests. Additionally, the strong scent of rosemary can confuse a variety of pests, protecting more vulnerable plants nearby. These aromatic herbs act as natural pest deterrents, reducing the need for chemical interventions and promoting a more organic gardening approach.

When considering which herbs to pair together or with other plants, it is essential to consider their growth requirements and how their presence might impact their companions. For example, chives and parsley can be planted together as they both thrive in full sun to partial shade and require similar watering schedules. This pairing not only conserves space but also creates a symbiotic relationship where each plant benefits from the proximity of the other. Chives can deter aphids and beetles, enhancing the growth environment for parsley. On the other hand, dill and fennel should not be planted together as they can cross-pollinate, potentially affecting the growth and quality of their seeds. Understanding these interactions is key to creating a balanced and productive herb garden.

Beyond their roles in pest management and garden aesthetics, many herbs also offer significant medicinal and culinary benefits, which can be a great addition to your home remedies and kitchen recipes. Mint, for instance, not only freshens the air but can also soothe stomach aches and relieve headaches when used in teas. Lavender, while known for its calming scent and ability to attract pollinators, can also be used to create essential oils or add a floral touch to baked goods. Incorporating these herbs into your garden means you have a ready supply of natural remedies and flavor enhancers just a few steps away from your kitchen.

Integrating herbs into your garden design can be both functional and aesthetically pleasing. When planning your herb garden, consider both the height and spread of each herb. Taller herbs like fennel can be used as a backdrop for lower-growing plants like thyme and oregano. This not only utilizes space efficiently but also creates a tiered effect in your garden, adding depth and variety to the landscape. Additionally, consider using herbs as border plants along garden paths or around vegetable patches. This not only helps define different areas of your garden but also ensures that the herbs are easily accessible for culinary or medicinal use. The strategic placement of herbs can transform the functionality and appearance of your garden, making it a more inviting and productive space.

By understanding and utilizing the dynamic relationships between herbs and other garden plants, you can create a more integrated and sustainable garden ecosystem. The thoughtful pairing of herbs not only enhances the health and productivity of your garden but also adds a layer of complexity to your gardening experience, offering endless possibilities for culinary, medicinal, and aesthetic uses. As you continue to explore and experiment with different herb pairings, you'll likely discover new and exciting ways to enhance both the beauty and functionality of your garden.

6.4 Flowers That Enhance Vegetable and Fruit Gardens

Integrating flowers into your vegetable and fruit gardens isn't just about adding splashes of color; these botanical beauties play crucial roles in enhancing the productivity and health of your garden. Flowers can attract an array of beneficial pollinators, naturally deter pests, and even contribute directly to your kitchen table as edible delights. By understanding which flowers to plant and how to position them among your vegetables and fruits, you can create a garden that is not only visually stunning but also ecologically vibrant and productive.

Attracting Pollinators with Flowers

Pollinators are vital to the success of many fruit and vegetable plants, as they significantly enhance the pollination process, leading to better fruit set and more bountiful harvests. Flowers such as zinnias, sunflowers, and lavender are powerhouses when it comes to attracting bees, butterflies, and other pollinating insects. Planting these flowers strategically throughout your garden can create pollinator hotspots, which ensure that these beneficial insects are regularly visiting and aiding in the pollination of your crops. For instance, placing clusters of bright, nectar-rich cosmos near tomato plants can increase bee activity around these crops, enhancing their pollination and resulting in more tomatoes. Similarly, sunflowers, with their large, pollen-laden heads, can attract bees and birds, which not only pollinate the sunflowers themselves but also other plants in the vicinity.

Flowers for Pest Control

Beyond their beauty and allure for pollinators, certain flowers also act as natural pest deterrents. Marigolds, for example, are renowned for their ability to repel nematodes and even some above-ground pests, such as whiteflies, when planted near sensitive crops like tomatoes or peppers. The strong scent of French marigolds, in particular, is believed to confuse pests and mask the smell of your vegetables, protecting them from being targeted. Another excellent choice for pest control is nasturtiums, which can serve as a trap crop for aphids. By planting them along the edges of your garden or near susceptible crops, they can draw aphids away, keeping your more valuable plants safe. Using these flowers strategically can reduce your need for chemical pesticides, leading to a healthier, more natural garden environment.

Edible Flowers

Many gardeners are delighted to discover that several ornamental flowers can also be culinary treasures. Edible flowers like calendula, nasturtiums, and borage not only add aesthetic value to your garden but also enhance your dishes with their unique flavors and colors. Calendula petals have a peppery taste and can be sprinkled over salads or used as a garnish, while nasturtiums, with their bright blooms, offer a burst of peppery zest and are perfect for adding a splash of color to salads. Borage flowers, with their cool, cucumber-like flavor, make a refreshing addition to drinks and summer dishes. Planting these flowers among your vegetables not only maximizes the use of your garden space but also brings an extra layer of flavor and creativity to your cooking.

Design Tips for Flower Integration

Designing a garden that incorporates flowers effectively requires consideration of both aesthetics and function. When integrating flowers for pollination and pest control, consider their height, bloom time, and color to create a visually appealing yet functional garden layout. For instance, taller flowers like sunflowers can create a stunning backdrop for lower-growing vegetables, while also attracting pollinators. Grouping flowers of various heights and colors can also add depth and interest to your garden, making it a more enjoyable and engaging space. Additionally, consider the blooming periods of your chosen flowers to ensure that there are always a few plants in bloom, providing a continuous attraction for pollinators and ongoing beauty for your garden.

Through the strategic use of flowers, your garden can become a robust ecosystem that supports a healthy balance of beauty, productivity, and biodiversity. The right flowers can transform your garden into a lively hub of pollinator activity, a fortress against pests, and a source of culinary inspiration. As you plant and watch these flowers grow, you'll find that they bring not only life and color to your garden but also a deeper connection to the natural world.

Reflecting on the Role of Flowers in the Garden

In this chapter, we explored the multifaceted roles that flowers can play in enhancing vegetable and fruit gardens. From attracting essential pollinators and providing natural pest control to adding edible beauty to your table, flowers are integral to creating a balanced and productive garden. As you integrate these floral companions into your garden, you'll notice not only the practical benefits but also the sheer joy that comes from gardening amidst such vibrant diversity. Looking ahead, the next chapter will delve into organic pest control methods, continuing our journey toward cultivating a healthy and sustainable garden environment. Here, we'll build on the natural strategies introduced through floral companionship, exploring more ways to protect and nurture your garden naturally.

Chapter 7:
Organic Pest Control

STEPPING INTO YOUR GARDEN, YOU might marvel at the lush greens and vibrant flowers, a testament to your dedication and love for gardening. Yet, lurking beneath this beauty can be the less welcome sight of garden pests, which threaten to undermine your hard work. It's a common plight many gardeners face, but before you reach for chemical solutions, consider a more harmonious approach: organic pest control through companion planting. This chapter delves into the natural strategies that can protect your garden, ensuring it remains a healthy and thriving ecosystem without the need for harsh chemicals.

7.1 Understanding Natural Pest Deterrence with Plants

How Plants Deter Pests

Nature, in its wisdom, has equipped plants with a variety of mechanisms to defend against pests, mechanisms that you can leverage to safeguard your garden. These natural defenses include a range of aromatic compounds that confuse or repel pests, bitter tastes that discourage feeding, and even physical barriers that prevent pests from accessing the plant. For instance, the strong scents emitted by herbs like lavender and rosemary can mask the smell of nearby plants, making it harder for pests to locate their preferred hosts. Similarly, the sharp taste of chives can deter animals like deer and rabbits from nibbling on more palatable vegetables nearby. Moreover, the hairy leaves of plants like borage can physically prevent pests such as caterpillars and aphids from comfortably settling and feeding.

List of Pest Deterrent Plants

To harness the power of these natural defenders, here's a detailed list of plants known for their pest-deterring abilities:

- *Marigolds:* These bright flowers are not just pretty to look at; they release a chemical into the soil that deters nematodes and can repel insects like whiteflies when planted around tomatoes or peppers.
- *Garlic:* Known for its strong scent, planting garlic can help repel pests such as aphids and borers from fruit trees and roses.
- *Basil:* The aromatic leaves of basil can confuse pests like thrips and mosquitoes, making it an excellent companion for vegetable crops such as tomatoes and lettuce.
- *Nasturtiums:* These vibrant flowers not only attract pollinators but also serve as a trap crop for aphids, drawing them away from more valuable plants.

Integrating Pest Deterrent Plants

To maximize the effectiveness of these pest-deterrent plants, strategic integration into your garden is crucial. Consider planting a border of marigolds around your vegetable garden to create a protective barrier against nematodes and other insects. Intersperse garlic throughout your rose garden to help deter pests that target these delicate flowers. Plant basil alongside your tomato plants not only for convenience when cooking but also to help keep some common pests at bay. By thoughtfully placing these plants where their protective properties can be most effective, you enhance your garden's natural resilience against pests.

Limitations and Considerations

While natural pest deterrence provides a more eco-friendly alternative to chemical pesticides, it's important to recognize its limitations and consider them in your garden planning. These natural methods may not offer immediate or complete control of pest populations as chemical solutions might. The effectiveness can also vary based on factors such as plant health, pest population size, and environmental conditions. Therefore, integrating these methods with other organic gardening practices, such as maintaining healthy soil, diversifying plant species in your garden, and encouraging beneficial insects, can help create a more comprehensive pest management strategy.

7.2 Plant Pairings to Combat Common Garden Pests

Navigating the challenges of garden pests can often feel like a game of strategy, where choosing the right plant allies makes all the difference. Through specific companion plant pairings, you can naturally deter or manage common garden pests, enhancing the health and productivity of your garden without resorting to chemical interventions. Let's explore some effective pairings that have been proven to keep pests at bay and examine how these strategies fit into an overall Integrated Pest Management (IPM) approach.

One exemplary pairing that has shown great success in deterring pests is the combination of tomatoes and borage. Borage not only enriches the soil with minerals but also wards off tomato hornworms, a common pest that can devastate tomato plants. Planting borage alongside your tomatoes provides a dual benefit; it enhances the flavor of the tomatoes while acting as a natural pest deterrent. Another strategic pairing involves using radishes to draw flea beetles away from cruciferous vegetables like broccoli and cabbage. Radishes act as a trap crop, attracting flea beetles to themselves and away from more valuable crops, thereby minimizing damage to your main harvest. This method not only reduces the pest load on crucial crops but also utilizes less valuable plants to safeguard your garden's productivity.

Reflecting on real-life applications of these strategies, consider the success story of a community garden that integrated aromatic herbs such as thyme and lavender around their vegetable plots. These herbs, known for their strong scents, effectively masked the smell of nearby vegetables, reducing the incidence of pest infestations. The gardeners noticed a significant decrease in the number of aphids and cabbage moths, which were previously a major concern. This example not only demonstrates the effectiveness of using aromatic herbs as pest deterrents but also highlights the importance of understanding pest behaviors and preferences in planning effective companion planting strategies.

Companion planting plays a crucial role in Integrated Pest Management (IPM), a holistic approach to pest control that emphasizes the use of natural and sustainable methods. IPM aims to manage pest populations at acceptable levels using environmentally sensitive strategies. By incorporating companion plants that deter or trap pests, you can reduce the reliance on chemical pesticides, which not only aligns with the sustainable goals of IPM but also helps preserve the ecological balance of your garden. For instance, employing marigolds to manage nematodes in the soil or using nasturtiums to attract aphids away from more valuable crops are methods that integrate seamlessly into an IPM strategy, offering natural solutions to pest challenges.

Moreover, certain plant pairings can attract natural predators of common pests, adding another layer of defense to your garden's pest management strategy. For example, planting a mix of flowering plants like daisies and alyssum can attract ladybugs and lacewings, known predators of aphids and other harmful insects. These beneficial predators help keep pest populations in check, reducing the need for manual intervention. By creating a habitat that supports these natural allies, you not only enhance the biodiversity of your garden but also leverage the natural ecological processes to maintain plant health and balance.

Through thoughtful selection and placement of companion plants, you can effectively manage garden pests in a way that enhances the health and yield of your garden while maintaining ecological integrity. This approach not only makes your garden a thriving, productive space but also a testament to the possibilities of natural pest management. As you continue to explore and implement these companion planting strategies, you'll find your garden not just surviving but thriving with a robust defense system powered by nature itself.

7.3 Companion Plants for Disease Prevention

One of the most disheartening challenges you might face in the quest for a flourishing garden is plant disease. Fungal infections and soil-borne diseases can swiftly turn a vibrant garden into a withering landscape. Fortunately, certain companion plants act as natural guardians against these ailments, enhancing the health and resilience of your garden without the need for chemical fungicides. Understanding which plants can help prevent diseases and how to strategically place them in your garden is essential for maintaining a robust garden ecosystem.

Plants That Prevent Fungal Diseases

Fungal diseases thrive in environments where air circulation is poor and moisture is excessive. Companion planting can play a crucial role in managing these conditions by incorporating plants that naturally inhibit fungal growth. For instance, garlic has antifungal properties that can help protect neighboring plants from diseases like powdery mildew and rust. Planting garlic near susceptible crops, such as tomatoes and roses, can create a protective barrier against these common fungal issues. Another powerful ally is chamomile, known not only for its soothing tea but also for its ability to prevent damping-off in seedlings—a fungal condition that causes young plants to rot at the base. Integrating chamomile throughout your nursery beds or greenhouse can safeguard your young plants during their most vulnerable stages. These plants work by changing the microclimate around them or producing compounds that inhibit fungal growth, offering a natural line of defense against plant diseases.

Spacing and Airflow Considerations

Proper spacing and ensuring good airflow around your plants are critical in preventing the onset and spread of diseases. Overcrowded plants can create a humid microclimate that is ideal for fungal and bacterial diseases to thrive. Companion planting can help manage plant density and improve air circulation, which is essential for keeping foliage dry and diseases at bay. For example, tall plants like corn can be spaced with lower-growing plants such as squash. This not only optimizes space but also ensures that air can flow freely around the plants, reducing the risk of diseases like leaf blight. Moreover, strategic planting of aromatic herbs such as mint or basil around more dense, bushy plants can help deter pests and improve air penetration, thanks to their less dense growth patterns and the natural movement they encourage when they release their scents.

Soil-Borne Disease Management

Soil-borne diseases often lurk in the garden unseen until they strike, causing root rot and other harmful conditions. Companion planting can be a strategic approach to managing these hidden dangers. Marigolds, for example, are not only cheerful and bright but also secrete substances that can kill nematodes and other harmful soil-dwelling organisms that cause root diseases. Planting marigolds as a cover crop or interspersed with vegetables like carrots and potatoes can significantly reduce the nematode populations in the soil. Additionally, rotating plants that add organic matter to the soil, such as beans and peas, can improve soil structure and drainage, helping to prevent waterlogging and root diseases. These legumes also fix nitrogen in the soil, which strengthens plant health and further enhances their ability to resist diseases.

Rotating Disease-Resistant Companions

Implementing a rotation of disease-resistant companion plants is a proactive strategy to maintain soil health and prevent the accumulation of pathogens. Plants vary in their susceptibility to diseases; by rotating them, you can avoid giving any particular soil-borne disease a continual host on which to thrive. For instance, after growing tomatoes, which are prone to verticillium and fusarium wilt, you can plant cereals like wheat or barley, which are not affected by these pathogens. This break in the cycle deprives the pathogens of their preferred hosts, reducing their presence in the soil. Following the cereals, planting brassicas like broccoli or kale, which can benefit from the organic matter left by the cereals, can be an excellent way to keep the soil healthy and disease-free. This rotation not only disrupts the disease cycle but also helps in maintaining the nutrient balance and structure of your garden soil, ensuring it remains fertile and productive.

By integrating these disease prevention strategies through companion planting, you empower your garden to defend itself against a variety of common ailments, reducing your dependency on chemical treatments. This approach not only keeps your garden healthier but also supports a more sustainable gardening practice, aligning with the natural ecological balances and cycles. As you continue to nurture and observe your garden, you'll find that these methods not only enhance the resilience of your plants but also deepen your connection to the natural world, enriching your gardening experience with every season.

7.4 Attracting Beneficial Insects to Your Garden

Imagine your garden as a bustling hub where every visitor plays a crucial role in maintaining its health and vitality. Among these visitors are beneficial insects, nature's own pest control agents and pollinators, who can significantly enhance the productivity and health of your garden. Understanding who these beneficial insects are and how to attract them can transform your garden into a thriving ecosystem, rich in biodiversity and low in pest populations.

Beneficial Insects 101

Beneficial insects in your garden can be broadly categorized into pollinators and predators. Pollinators, such as bees and butterflies, are vital for the reproduction of many plants, helping you achieve a successful harvest of fruits, vegetables, and seeds. Predatory insects, like ladybugs, lacewings, and hoverflies, serve as natural pest control, devouring aphids, mites, and other pests that can damage your plants. Welcoming these insects into your garden not only supports their populations but also contributes to a balanced ecosystem where chemical pesticides can become a thing of the past.

Plants That Attract Beneficial Insects

To invite these helpful creatures into your garden, consider planting a variety of flora that appeal to them. Flowers such as alyssum, sunflowers, and cosmos are irresistible to many beneficial insects due to their abundant nectar and pollen. Herbs like dill, fennel, and coriander can attract predatory insects by offering shelter and alternative food sources in the form of small insects that feed on these plants. Additionally, incorporating native plants into your garden is particularly effective as these plants have already been adapted to attract local insect populations. Creating a diverse planting scheme ensures that beneficial insects have resources throughout the growing season, keeping them returning to your garden as a reliable habitat.

Designing a Garden for Beneficial Insects

Designing your garden to maximize the presence of beneficial insects involves more than just planting the right plants. It's about creating an environment that supports their lifecycle. For instance, include areas of undisturbed soil and mulch where some predatory insects can nest and overwinter. Consider also the structure of your plantings; layered plant heights mimic natural habitats and provide shelters for insects from predators and harsh weather. A water source, such as a shallow dish filled with stones and water, will also attract and sustain these insects. By thinking about the needs of beneficial insects at every stage of their life, you can design a garden that is not only beautiful but also brimming with life.

Maintaining a Balanced Ecosystem

The key to maintaining a balanced garden ecosystem lies in the diversity of plant life and the practice of organic gardening methods. Avoiding the use of broad-spectrum pesticides, which can harm beneficial insects, is crucial. Instead, focus on targeted interventions, such as removing pests by hand or using barriers to protect plants. Regular monitoring of insect populations in your garden will help you understand whether your efforts to attract beneficial insects are effective and whether these populations are in balance with the rest of your garden's ecosystem. This mindful approach ensures that your garden not only thrives in terms of plant health but also supports a vibrant community of insects that contribute to its resilience and productivity.

As we wrap up this exploration of how to attract and support beneficial insects in your garden, remember that each step you take to welcome these natural allies plays a crucial role in developing a sustainable and thriving garden. From choosing the right plants to designing an insect-friendly garden layout, each decision contributes to a healthier garden ecosystem. As you implement these strategies, you'll find that your reliance on chemical interventions decreases, and your garden becomes a more vibrant and self-regulating environment. This chapter sets the stage for the next, where we'll delve into optimizing your garden for pollination and productivity, ensuring that every plant, from flowers to vegetables, reaches its full potential.

Chapter 8:
Optimizing Pollination and Productivity

I MAGINE YOUR GARDEN AS A bustling city during rush hour, where every bit of activity contributes to the overall vibrancy and function of the ecosystem. In this urban analogy, pollinators are the commuters, essential for the flow and productivity of your garden. Their tireless work ensures that plants are pollinated, leading to fruitful harvests and a healthy, thriving garden. In this chapter, I'll guide you through creating a sanctuary that invites these crucial garden allies to visit more often and stay longer.

8.1 Plants That Attract Pollinators

Pollinators, such as bees, butterflies, and hummingbirds, are vital to your garden's success. They transfer pollen from one flower to another, facilitating the growth of fruits and seeds. A garden buzzing with pollinators is a sign of a healthy environment, but achieving this requires more than just luck. It involves planting specific varieties that attract these beneficial visitors and arranging your space to welcome and sustain them.

Key Pollinator Plants

The first step is to know which plants are irresistible to pollinators. Flowers with bright colors and rich nectar, like lavender, sunflowers, and zinnias, are pollinator magnets. Herbs such as rosemary, thyme, and mint also attract bees with their aromatic blossoms. It's not just about choosing the right plants; placement is crucial, too. For example, planting sunflowers in a spot that gets ample sunlight not only ensures healthy growth but also maximizes visibility to attract more bees. Similarly, clustering small flowers like lavender and thyme creates a "target" for pollinators, making your garden an easier and more attractive destination.

Creating a Pollinator-Friendly Garden

To make your garden a haven for pollinators, consider their lifecycle needs. This includes providing sources of water, like a shallow birdbath or a dripping faucet, which can offer a much-needed drink to busy pollinators. Incorporating features like rocks for butterflies to sunbathe or undisturbed patches of bare earth for ground-nesting bees can make your garden more inviting. Diversity in plant selection also plays a crucial role. By planting a variety of flowering plants that bloom at different times of the year, you ensure a continuous supply of food, which can encourage pollinators to remain in your garden throughout the growing season.

Seasonal Pollinator Support

Supporting pollinators year-round requires planning. Early spring flowers like crocus and hyacinth provide the first nectar sources for bees coming out of hibernation. Summer blooms, such as coneflowers and bee balm, keep the momentum going, while late bloomers like asters and goldenrod ensure that pollinators have sustenance as they prepare for winter. This continuous bloom strategy not only supports a wider range of pollinators but also adds ongoing color and interest to your garden.

Pollinator Habitats

Creating dedicated habitats can significantly boost the number of pollinators that visit your garden. This might involve constructing features like bee hotels, which offer shelter to solitary bees. You can make these from untreated wood or hollow bamboo stems. For butterflies, consider planting a butterfly bush or creating a muddy puddle area, which provides essential minerals and a breeding ground for these delicate creatures. Designing your garden with these habitats in mind turns it into a sanctuary for pollinators, ensuring their health and your garden's productivity.

8.2 Techniques to Increase Pollination in Your Garden

Ensuring your garden is a hot spot for pollination involves more than just planting the right flowers; it's about actively engaging in practices that enhance the pollination process. One such practice is hand pollination, a straightforward yet effective technique especially useful for plants like squash, cucumbers, and melons, which might not attract enough natural pollinators. Hand pollination can significantly increase the yield and ensure the fruits develop properly. To hand pollinate, first identify the male and female flowers; male flowers generally have a straight stem and a pollen-covered anther, while female flowers have a swollen base that looks like a miniature version of the fruit. Using a small brush or even your fingertip, gently transfer pollen from the male flower to the stigma in the center of the female flower. This mimicry of natural pollinator activity can be particularly rewarding when you see your plants thriving and producing abundantly.

Maximizing natural pollination involves strategic thinking about the plant layout and variety in your garden. Designing your garden so that it is accessible and attractive to pollinators can make a significant difference. For example, planting in clusters can create a "target" for pollinators, making it easier for them to find the flowers. Including a range of plants that bloom at different times ensures that pollinators have a reason to keep coming back throughout the growing season. Furthermore, incorporating plants with various flower shapes and sizes caters to different types of pollinators, with some preferring the deep blooms of foxgloves and others the flat, composite flowers of daisies.

Encouraging frequent visits from pollinators also means creating an environment that meets their needs for water and shelter. Pollinators need water just as much as your plants do, but in a way that they can access safely. A shallow water source, such as a birdbath with stones or marbles for them to land on, can provide this vital resource without the risk of drowning. Providing shelter, such as hedgerows or undisturbed grassy areas where pollinators can hide from predators or take refuge from adverse weather, can also encourage them to stay in your garden longer. By ensuring these basic needs are met, you make your garden a more appealing and supportive space for pollinators.

Finally, prioritizing the health and safety of pollinators is paramount. This means avoiding the use of pesticides, which can be harmful or even lethal to them. If pest control is necessary, opt for targeted, natural solutions that do not harm pollinators. For instance, using insecticidal soap on aphid-infested plants can be effective, but it should be applied in the evening when bees are less active to minimize their risk. Creating a garden that is safe for pollinators helps protect these essential creatures. It contributes to the sustainability and productivity of your gardening efforts, ensuring that your plants are pollinated effectively and can produce to their fullest potential. By integrating these strategies into your gardening practices, you actively enhance the pollination process, leading to a more productive and vibrant garden.

8.3 Maximizing Harvest with Companion Planting

In your garden's lush tapestry, each plant not only contributes to the aesthetic but also plays a vital role in the collective productivity of the space. Imagine your garden as a team, where each member supports the other, not just living side by side but actively enhancing each other's performance. This is the essence of companion planting, a method that, when utilized effectively, can significantly boost the fruit and vegetable set, enhance nutrient sharing, reduce resource competition, and optimize harvest scheduling.

Boosting Fruit and Vegetable Set

One of the most remarkable benefits of companion planting is its ability to increase the yield of your fruits and vegetables. This happens through various natural interactions between the plants. For instance, the presence of certain flowers can increase pollination rates for fruit-bearing plants. Marigolds, with their bright, inviting blooms, attract bees and other pollinators, thus enhancing the pollination of nearby crops like cucumbers and tomatoes, leading to a better set of fruits. Similarly, the strategic placement of aromatic herbs such as basil near tomato plants has improved their growth and fruit production. The strong scent of basil helps repel harmful insects and may even attract beneficial ones, ensuring that your tomatoes are pollinated well and less stressed by pests. This symbiotic relationship not only maximizes the productivity of the space but also ensures that plants produce fruits and vegetables at their peak potential.

Nutrient Sharing Among Companions

The underground world of your garden is a bustling hub of activity where roots intertwine and microorganisms thrive, facilitating the complex process of nutrient uptake and sharing. Companion planting can enhance this process. Take, for example, the classic pairing of corn and beans. Corn, a tall plant, acts as a natural trellis for the climbing beans, which, being legumes, have the ability to fix atmospheric nitrogen into the soil. This nitrogen is then readily available for the corn, which requires high amounts of nitrogen to grow. This mutual exchange ensures both plants have access to the necessary nutrients, enhancing their growth and productivity. Similarly, deep-rooted plants like carrots can help bring nutrients up from lower soil layers, making them available to shallow-rooted companions like lettuce, enhancing the overall fertility of the soil.

Reducing Competition

Selecting companion plants that do not compete with each other for resources is crucial for their mutual survival and growth. This involves understanding the root systems, nutrient needs, and growth patterns of each plant. For instance, pairing deep-rooted plants with those that have shallow root systems can optimize the use of soil space and nutrients. Radishes, which grow quickly and have shallow roots, can be planted next to carrots, which take longer to mature and have deeper roots. This arrangement prevents the two from competing for the same soil space and nutrients. Additionally, understanding light requirements can help in arranging plants so that taller ones provide necessary shade to those that thrive in cooler, less intense light conditions without out-competing them for sunlight.

Harvest Scheduling

To ensure a continuous and efficient harvest, it's essential to plan the planting and harvesting phases of your garden carefully. Companion planting offers a strategic advantage by allowing you to stagger your crops' maturity, ensuring that not all plants need to be harvested at the same time, which can be overwhelming and impractical. For example, fast-growing vegetables like spinach can be harvested just a few weeks after planting, while slower-maturing vegetables like broccoli are still developing. This method not only extends your garden's productivity period but also reduces waste, as you can harvest and consume fresh produce according to your needs. Additionally, some plants can be harvested multiple times, like leafy greens, which can be cut and come again, providing a yield throughout the season while their companions mature at their own pace.

By implementing these companion planting strategies, you effectively create a garden that is more than just a collection of individual plants. It becomes a cohesive unit where each plant contributes to the success of the others, leading to a more productive, sustainable, and harmonious garden environment. As you continue to experiment and learn from the interactions within your garden, you'll find that companion planting not only makes ecological sense but also brings a sense of connection and satisfaction as you watch your garden elements work together, thriving in unison.

8.4 Seasonal Companion Planting for Year-Round Harvests

The dream of harvesting fresh produce from your garden throughout the year can become a reality with strategic planning and clever plant selection. To achieve a garden that continuously produces, you'll need to think beyond the traditional growing seasons and consider how you can extend your gardening activities. This approach involves careful timing and choosing plant varieties that thrive under varying conditions, ensuring that your garden beds remain vibrant and productive from January to December.

Planning for Continuous Harvest

Creating a garden that yields produce year-round starts with understanding the different growing conditions each season presents and planning your planting schedule accordingly. Start by dividing the year into the main seasonal segments: spring, summer, fall, and winter. Each season has its champions; for instance, leafy greens and certain herbs can survive the chill of early spring, while root vegetables like carrots and beets are perfect for late fall harvesting. Summer, of course, is ideal for warm-weather crops like tomatoes, peppers, and cucumbers. By planting a variety of crops that have staggered maturing times within these seasons, you can ensure that as one crop is being harvested, another is developing. Additionally, consider using succession planting—sowing seeds at intervals—within each season to avoid all crops maturing at once, which not only spreads out your harvest but also minimizes the risk of losing all your produce to pests, disease, or adverse weather at once.

Winter Companion Planting

Contrary to popular belief, the colder months don't necessarily mean the end of your gardening. With the right strategies, you can continue to grow and harvest even in winter. Utilizing structures like greenhouses or cold frames can protect your plants from harsh conditions and provide a microclimate that supports growth. Winter-hardy varieties such as kale, Swiss chard, and some types of lettuce can thrive in these environments, giving you fresh greens even when the ground outside is frozen. Furthermore, indoor gardening can be an excellent alternative during the coldest months. Herbs like basil and cilantro can grow well on sunny windowsills, providing fresh flavors for your winter meals. By integrating these approaches, your garden can remain productive and inspiring throughout the winter months, defying the dormant landscape often associated with this season.

Transitioning Between Seasons

Smooth transitions between seasons are crucial to maintaining a year-round productive garden. This involves not only physical preparation, such as cleaning up spent plants and replenishing mulch, but also strategic planning. As one season begins to wane, start preparing for the next by germinating seeds indoors or protecting late-season crops with row covers. Adjust your watering routines to match the changing weather conditions, and be vigilant about pest and disease control, as these can often proliferate during transitional periods. Additionally, keep a garden journal to record what works and what doesn't, as this information will be invaluable in planning future garden transitions. This ongoing cycle of preparation and adaptation ensures that your garden remains dynamic and productive, seamlessly flowing from one season into the next.

Case Studies of Year-Round Gardens

Real-world examples can provide inspiration and practical insights into managing a garden that produces all year round. Consider the case of an urban gardener who transformed her rooftop into a thriving vegetable garden. By using raised beds and portable greenhouses, she was able to grow a variety of vegetables, such as tomatoes, peppers and greens throughout the year. Each season, she adjusted her crop selection and utilized protective coverings to extend the growing season into the colder months. Another example is a community garden in a temperate climate that utilized extensive mulching and cold-hardy plant varieties to keep their garden productive through the winter. These examples showcase how adaptability, coupled with a deep understanding of the local climate and ecosystem, can lead to successful year-round gardening.

By embracing the principles of seasonal companion planting and learning from successful case studies, you can transform your garden into a year-round source of fresh produce. This not only maximizes your garden's potential but also brings a sense of achievement and continuity to your gardening efforts. As we conclude this exploration of year-round gardening, remember that each season offers unique opportunities and challenges. Embracing this cyclical nature can lead to a deeper connection with your garden and the rhythms of the natural world.

In the next chapter, we will explore common mistakes in companion planting and how to avoid them, ensuring your garden not only survives but thrives under your care. This knowledge will help you refine your techniques and enhance the resilience and productivity of your garden.

Chapter 9:
Common Mistakes and How to Avoid Them

I N THE VERDANT WORLD OF gardening, each mistake is a stepping stone to mastery, an opportunity to learn and grow alongside your garden. As you cultivate your green space, understanding the common pitfalls can significantly enhance your gardening experience. This chapter is dedicated to guiding you through some of the frequent hiccups gardeners encounter with companion planting, ensuring your garden is not just a patch of soil but a thriving ecosystem of harmoniously interacting plants.

9.1 Why Your Companion Planting Might Fail: Common Pitfalls

Misunderstanding Plant Relationships

The intricate dance of companion planting is based on the relationships between plants—some are friends, others, unfortunately, are foes. A classic misstep is pairing plants together without understanding their specific interactions. For example, while beans generally flourish when planted with carrots, planting them near onions can inhibit their growth due to onions' allelopathic properties, which can hinder the growth of certain plants. This misunderstanding can lead to reduced yields and even plant fatalities. To avoid this, it's crucial to research plant compatibilities thoroughly before planting. A handy method to keep track of friendly and unfriendly pairings is to create a companion planting chart, which you can refer to when planning your garden layout. This proactive approach ensures that each of your garden residents supports rather than sabotages its neighbors.

Ignoring Soil Requirements

Soil is not just dirt—it's a living, breathing foundation that nourishes your garden. Each plant has unique soil preferences, and overlooking these can lead to less-than-ideal growth conditions. For instance, blueberries thrive in acidic soil, while cabbages prefer a more neutral pH. When these plants are placed in incompatible soil types without proper adjustment, they struggle to absorb nutrients effectively, which can stunt their growth and reduce their resilience against pests and diseases. To foster a thriving garden, it's essential to perform a soil test before planting. This test will reveal the pH level and nutrient profile of your soil, allowing you to amend it accordingly. Adding organic matter, such as compost or leaf mold, can also improve soil structure and nutrient content, creating a robust environment for your plants to flourish.

Overcrowding Plants

In their enthusiasm to grow a lush garden, beginners often plant too closely, not accounting for the mature size of the plants. Overcrowding can lead to fierce competition for light, water, and nutrients, significantly stressing the plants and making them more susceptible to diseases and insect attacks. Furthermore, poor air circulation in a cramped garden can invite fungal diseases like powdery mildew. The key to avoiding this pitfall is to follow spacing guidelines, which are often provided on seed packets or in gardening guides. Additionally, practicing vertical gardening by using trellises for climbing plants like cucumbers and beans can maximize your garden space and improve air circulation, helping keep your plants healthy and productive.

Neglecting Pest and Disease Management

Even the best-planned companion gardens can fall victim to pests and diseases if preventive measures are not implemented. Relying solely on companion planting for pest control might not always suffice, especially when pest populations are high. Regular monitoring of your garden is crucial for early detection and management of potential issues. Introducing beneficial insects, such as ladybugs and lacewings, can naturally reduce pest populations. Additionally, applying organic mulches can suppress soil-borne diseases and improve plant health. For persistent pest or disease problems, organic pesticides like neem oil can be used as a last resort. However, these should be applied judiciously to avoid harming beneficial insects and the overall soil health.

By understanding and addressing these common pitfalls, you can enhance the harmony and productivity of your companion garden. Each plant, when properly supported, contributes to a dynamic, healthy garden ecosystem, reducing the need for chemical interventions and creating a sustainable, vibrant outdoor space. As you continue to nurture and refine your gardening practices, remember that each challenge is an opportunity to learn and grow, not just for your plants, but for you as a gardener.

9.2 Addressing Soil Fertility Issues in Companion Planting

A thriving garden starts from the ground up, literally. The fertility of your soil is the cornerstone of your garden's health, influencing everything from plant growth to how well your companion planting strategies work. Recognizing the signs of poor soil fertility is crucial, as it allows you to take steps to improve conditions before your plants suffer irreversible damage. Visual cues such as stunted growth, yellowing leaves, and poor flowering or fruiting can all indicate that your plants are struggling due to inadequate soil nutrients. Each symptom points to different deficiencies: yellow leaves often suggest a lack of nitrogen, while weak stems or slow growth might indicate a phosphorus shortage. Observing your plants regularly helps you catch these signs early, enabling timely interventions that can dramatically improve your garden's vitality.

Once you've identified potential fertility issues, the next step is to improve your soil organically. The beauty of organic gardening lies in its sustainability and the robustness it brings to your garden ecosystem. Integrating organic matter into your soil is one of the simplest yet most effective ways to enhance its fertility. Materials like compost, decomposed leaves, or well-aged manure not only add essential nutrients back into the soil but also improve its structure, enhancing root growth and water retention. Composting is particularly rewarding as it allows you to recycle kitchen scraps and garden waste, turning what would be trash into valuable food for your garden. Creating your own compost pile might seem daunting at first, but it's quite straightforward and becomes second nature with a little practice. The key is to balance 'greens' such as vegetable peelings, which provide nitrogen, with 'browns' like dried leaves, which supply carbon. This balance helps the pile decompose effectively, creating rich compost that will nourish your plants.

The role of cover crops in maintaining soil fertility cannot be overstated. Plants like clover, vetch, and rye are not just placeholders in your garden during the off-season; they play a crucial role in soil health. These crops help fix nitrogen from the air into the soil, making it available for future plants. They also help prevent erosion, suppress weeds, and improve soil structure as their roots break up compacted ground and their decaying matter adds organic content to the soil. Planting cover crops during fallow periods keeps your garden productive even when it's not filled with vegetables and flowers, ensuring that when planting season comes around, your soil is in peak condition. For instance, planting clover in early fall after you've harvested your summer vegetables can provide numerous benefits. As a legume, clover fixes nitrogen, and when tilled into the soil in spring, it becomes a green manure, offering a nutrient-rich amendment for the next planting season.

Regular soil testing is the final piece of the puzzle in managing soil fertility. While observations and organic amendments go a long way, precise soil tests provide the detailed information you need to tailor your soil management practices accurately. These tests reveal not just pH but also detailed nutrient levels and other soil characteristics like organic matter content and cation exchange capacity, which affects the soil's ability to hold onto essential nutrients. Kits are available for home testing, but for the most comprehensive results, sending a soil sample to a local extension service or a professional soil-testing laboratory is advisable. This should ideally be done every couple of years, as soil properties can change depending on what you've planted, the amendments you've used, and even the weather. With these detailed insights, you can make informed decisions about what amendments your garden might need, avoiding the guesswork and waste associated with unnecessary or incorrect fertilization.

By taking these proactive steps towards managing soil fertility, you not only ensure that your plants have the best foundation for growth but also contribute to the sustainability and productivity of your garden. Healthy soil leads to healthy plants, which leads to a bountiful harvest, all interlinked in the beautiful cycle of gardening.

9.3 Managing Watering Challenges in Diverse Plantings

In the vibrant tapestry of your companion garden, maintaining the right moisture balance is akin to conducting an orchestra where each plant's water needs must harmonize perfectly with its neighbors. Understanding these needs and implementing efficient watering systems are essential steps to ensure every plant, from the thirst-quenching tomatoes to the drought-tolerant lavender, thrives in unison, without a single one suffering from too much or too little water.

The first step in this delicate balancing act is to accurately gauge the individual water requirements of your plants. This understanding begins with recognizing that not all plants thirst equally; some, like cucumbers and celery, are water lovers, requiring consistent moisture to flourish, while others, such as rosemary and sage, thrive in drier conditions. The key is to group plants with similar watering needs together. This strategy not only simplifies your watering routine but also prevents the overwatering or underwatering that can stress plants, making them more susceptible to diseases and poor growth. For instance, planting all your leafy greens in one bed allows you to water them heavily without worrying about the succulents nearby that prefer a drier soil. Observing your plants regularly helps you tune into their specific signs of water distress. Wilting, for example, might indicate immediate water needs, while yellowing leaves could suggest overwatering.

Once you are attuned to the varied needs of your garden's inhabitants, the next logical step is to install an efficient watering system that caters to these needs without waste. Drip irrigation systems and soaker hoses are excellent for this purpose. Drip irrigation delivers water directly to the base of the plant, minimizing evaporation and ensuring that water goes exactly where it's needed — the roots. It's particularly beneficial in a diverse planting setup where each plant's root zone might require different moisture levels. Soaker hoses, which allow water to seep out slowly along their length, are ideal for long, straight rows of plants and are excellent for conserving water. Both systems can be adjusted according to the watering needs of different garden sections and can be put on timers to ensure water is delivered at the most effective times, usually during the cooler parts of the day, to reduce evaporation losses.

Mulching stands out as another pivotal practice in managing soil moisture. A good layer of organic mulch, such as straw, bark, or shredded leaves, can dramatically reduce water evaporation from the soil, keeping it moist longer. Mulch also helps regulate soil temperature, keeping roots cool during hot spells and warm during cold snaps. Additionally, as organic mulches slowly decompose, they contribute to the organic matter in the soil, improving its water retention capacity and overall health. When applying mulch, ensure it's spread evenly around plants, leaving some space around the stem to prevent rot and fungal infections. This practice not only maintains optimal soil moisture but also adds to the overall vitality of the soil, supporting the lush growth of your garden.

Dealing with water competition among plants, especially in a densely planted bed, requires a thoughtful approach to spacing and grouping. Proper spacing allows each plant enough soil volume to explore water without having to compete aggressively with its neighbors. This can be particularly challenging in companion planting, where different species are grown together for mutual benefits. One way to manage this is by carefully planning plant heights and root depths in your companion planting scheme. Taller plants with deeper roots can be paired with shorter plants with shallow roots, ensuring they access different soil strata for moisture and reducing competition. Another effective method is to use plants that naturally retain water or create shade for the soil, such as squash plants, whose large leaves shade the ground, keeping it cool and reducing evaporation.

By integrating these strategies—understanding plant water needs, utilizing efficient irrigation systems, applying mulch, and thoughtful plant grouping—you create a garden environment where water is no longer a source of stress but a well-managed resource. This not only ensures the health and productivity of your garden but also conserves water, aligning your gardening practice with principles of sustainability and care for the planet. As you continue to refine these techniques, your garden will not only survive but thrive, showcasing the beauty and efficiency of a well-watered and lovingly tended ecosystem.

9.4 Overcoming Shade and Sunlight Imbalances

In the diverse ecosystem of your garden, light plays a pivotal role, akin to water and soil, in determining the health and productivity of your plants. Just as in a community where every individual needs adequate space to thrive, each plant in your garden requires its rightful share of sunlight to flourish. Yet, not all areas of a garden receive equal light due to natural shading from trees, buildings, or even other plants. This section will guide you through assessing light conditions, choosing shade-tolerant companions, adjusting plant layouts, and creatively using reflective surfaces to manage light distribution effectively in your garden.

Assessing Light Conditions

The first step in mastering light management in your garden is to conduct a thorough assessment of light conditions throughout the day. This involves observing which areas receive full sun, partial shade, or full shade at different times. A simple method is to take photos of your garden at various times—morning, noon, and late afternoon—to visually map out the sunlight distribution. You can also use a sun calculator tool, which provides a detailed analysis of sun exposure in your garden based on your specific location. Understanding these patterns allows you to make informed decisions about where to place certain plants. For example, vegetables like tomatoes and peppers thrive in full sun, needing at least six hours of direct sunlight daily, while ferns and hostas perform well in shaded areas.

Choosing Shade-Tolerant Companions

When dealing with shaded areas in your garden, selecting the right plants can make all the difference. Shade-tolerant plants are not only survivors in low-light conditions but can also add beauty and variety to these garden spots. Consider incorporating plants like astilbe, impatiens, and bleeding heart, which flourish in partial to full shade, offering vibrant colors and varied textures. These plants can be paired with taller, sun-loving plants that might cast shade below. For instance, planting shade-loving impatiens around the base of sun-thirsty sunflowers can optimize the use of vertical space and light, ensuring that both plant types receive their ideal lighting conditions without interfering with each other's growth.

Adjusting Plant Layouts

Skillful arrangement of plants can significantly enhance light efficiency in your garden. Start by positioning taller plants on the north side of your garden to prevent them from casting shadows on shorter plants. Utilize tiered planting designs where medium-height plants are placed in front of taller ones, and shorter or ground-cover plants are placed in the forefront. This stair-step arrangement ensures that all plants get adequate light without overshadowing one another. Furthermore, consider the angle of light during different seasons; the sun is lower in the sky during early spring and late fall, so be mindful of how seasonal changes affect light availability in your garden.

Utilizing Reflective Surfaces

An innovative way to enhance light in shaded areas is by using reflective surfaces to redirect sunlight. This can be particularly useful in urban gardens where buildings might block direct sunlight for parts of the day. Placing reflective materials, such as mirrors, shiny metal sheets, or even white-painted walls near your plants can help bounce additional light onto them. Ensure that these surfaces are positioned to reflect morning or late afternoon light, which is less intense and less likely to scorch your plants. This method can be especially effective for light-loving herbs and vegetables that might otherwise struggle in a garden with variable light conditions.

Managing light in your garden with thoughtful strategies ensures that every plant, regardless of its position, receives the love and light it needs to contribute to the lush, vibrant tableau of your green space. By assessing the specific light needs of your plants and creatively adjusting your garden layout and utilizing reflective materials, you can overcome the challenges of shade and sunlight imbalances. This not only leads to healthier plants but also maximizes the aesthetic and productive potential of every inch of your garden.

As we wrap up this exploration of light management in companion planting, remember that each step you take to optimize sunlight exposure is crucial for the overall health and success of your garden. These strategies, from assessing light conditions to creatively using reflective surfaces, empower you to create a more resilient and vibrant garden landscape. Next, we will delve into the art and science of plant nutrition, exploring how to nourish your plants for optimum health and productivity. This upcoming chapter will build on the foundational knowledge you've gained here, taking you deeper into the transformative practice of gardening.

Chapter 10:
Seasonal Care and Maintenance

IMAGINE THE FIRST WARM BREEZE of spring gently brushing against your face, a reminder that the earth is waking up from its winter slumber. This is a signal, not just to the natural world, but to you, the gardener, that it's time to prepare your companion garden for the upcoming growing season. Spring in the garden is a time of renewal and rebirth, but it also calls for thoughtful preparation and strategic planning. It's the perfect moment to lay the groundwork that will ensure a lush, thriving garden throughout the warmer months.

10.1   Spring Preparation for Your Companion Garden

Early Soil Preparation

As the frost begins to thaw and the soil becomes workable, your first task is to prepare the bedrock of your garden—its soil. Start by testing the soil to determine its pH and nutrient levels. This can be easily done with a home testing kit available at most garden centers. Understanding your soil's condition is crucial because it tells you exactly what amendments it might need. If, for instance, the soil is too acidic, incorporating some lime might be necessary; if it's lacking in nutrients, a good quality compost or well-rotted manure can replenish it.

Once you know what your soil needs, it's time to get your hands dirty. Turn the soil gently with a spade or a fork to loosen it, being careful not to disturb any beneficial microorganisms too much. This aeration is vital as it helps to improve drainage and allows new plant roots to penetrate more easily. If you're adding amendments, now is the time to mix them evenly throughout the soil. Another beneficial technique is to warm the soil before planting, which can be especially helpful in cooler climates. Covering your garden beds with black plastic or a similar material a few weeks before planting can raise the soil temperature, ensuring that your tender young plants will have a cozy start to life.

Choosing Spring Companions

When selecting plants for early spring planting, opt for those that can withstand a nip in the air. Hardy vegetables, like peas, spinach, and kale, or herbs, such as parsley and cilantro, are excellent choices as they can handle cooler temperatures and even a light frost. When considering companion planting, think about the relationships between these plants. Peas, for example, fix nitrogen in the soil, which can be beneficial for leafy greens like spinach that require nitrogen-rich soil to flourish.

In your planning, also consider the height, spread, and root depth of your chosen plants to ensure they won't compete fiercely for space and resources. For example, planting taller peas along a trellis with lower-growing spinach at their base can create a microclimate that benefits both, with the peas providing some shade and cooler soil conditions for the spinach as the season warms.

Pest and Disease Prevention

Early prevention is key in managing pests and diseases in your garden. Begin by clearing out any leftover plant debris from the previous season, as this can harbor pests and diseases over the winter. Inspect your garden tools and containers to ensure they are clean and free from potential contaminants— a simple rinse with a solution of one part bleach to nine parts water can effectively disinfect your gardening equipment.

For companion planting, consider including plants that naturally repel pests or enhance the growth and flavor of their neighbors. Marigolds, for example, not only add a splash of color to your garden but also release a substance that deters nematodes and other pests. Garlic planted near roses can help prevent aphids, and chives can boost the growth and flavor of carrots while deterring carrot flies.

Pruning and Cleanup

Spring cleanup also involves pruning any overwintered plants. Remove dead or diseased branches to rejuvenate plants and encourage new growth. This not only improves the appearance of your plants but also opens their structure to better air circulation, which is vital in preventing fungal diseases. Pruning should be done with clean, sharp tools to make precise cuts that heal quickly.

Clearing winter mulch and replacing it with a fresh layer can also protect new plants from sudden temperature drops and keep the soil moist as temperatures begin to rise. This is also an ideal time to establish new mulch around young seedlings, which helps suppress weeds and retain soil moisture during the crucial early stages of growth.

As you engage in these spring preparations, remember that each step you take now lays the foundation for the lush growth to come. Your hands, caked in soil, and your garden, dotted with new sprouts, are clear signs that you are ready to grow alongside your garden. This active engagement not only prepares your garden for the season ahead but also reconnects you with the earth, a fundamental aspect of gardening that nourishes both the garden and the gardener's soul.

10.2   Summer Care: Watering, Weeding, and Monitoring

As the summer sun climbs higher and the days grow longer, your garden enters a period of vigorous growth, vibrant blooms, and bountiful harvests. This season, while beautiful, brings its own set of challenges that require diligent care and attention to ensure your plants not only survive but thrive in the heat. A key aspect of summer care in your companion garden is maintaining consistent watering practices. During these warmer months, the importance of providing your plants with deep, regular watering cannot be overstated. Unlike light, frequent sprinklings, deep watering encourages the roots of your plants to grow downward, seeking moisture and nutrients, which in turn helps them become more resilient and less susceptible to drought. Ideally, watering early in the morning is most effective as it allows the water to reach the roots before the heat of the day causes evaporation. For those with busy schedules, consider implementing a drip irrigation system that can be set on a timer to ensure your plants receive water at the optimal time. This method not only conserves water but also delivers it directly to the base of the plant, minimizing waste and reducing the spread of leaf diseases that can occur when foliage remains wet.

Weed management during the summer is another crucial aspect of keeping your garden healthy. Weeds can be particularly aggressive in the warm weather, competing with your plants for water, sunlight, and nutrients. To manage them effectively, adopting a non-invasive approach that protects your companion plantings is essential. Mulching proves to be an invaluable strategy here. Applying a thick layer of organic mulch, such as straw, shredded bark, or leaf mold, around your plants can significantly suppress weed growth by blocking light from reaching the soil surface. Additionally, mulch helps retain soil moisture and keeps the root systems cool, which is vital during hot weather. Hand-pulling weeds can also be effective, especially if done regularly before they have a chance to establish or go to seed. Be gentle when pulling weeds around your companion plants to avoid disturbing their roots, and always aim to get the entire root system out to prevent regrowth.

Monitoring for pests and diseases is another key task that needs your regular attention throughout the summer. Many pests and diseases thrive in warm weather, and early detection is critical to managing them effectively. Regularly inspect your plants for signs of distress, such as unusual spots on leaves, distorted growth, or visible pests like aphids and beetles. Implementing organic control options can effectively address these issues without resorting to harsh chemicals. For instance, introducing beneficial insects such as ladybugs can naturally reduce the population of aphids. Neem oil, a natural pesticide, can be used to tackle a range of pests and fungal diseases without harming your plants or the beneficial insects within your garden ecosystem. Always apply treatments in the evening to minimize the impact on pollinators and to increase the effectiveness of the application, as UV light can break down organic treatments.

Succession planting is a dynamic strategy you can employ during summer to ensure a continuous harvest. This practice involves planting new seeds at intervals throughout the growing season so that as one crop matures and is harvested, another begins to grow. For example, once you harvest early lettuce, replant the space with a quick-growing crop like radishes or turnips. Not only does this method maximize the use of your garden space, but it also keeps your soil covered, which helps to maintain its structure and nutrient content. Succession planting requires a bit of planning to ensure that your timing aligns with crop maturity dates and seasonal changes. Keeping a garden calendar can help you track planting and harvesting times, making it easier to know when to sow new seeds to keep your garden productive throughout the season.

10.3   Fall Tasks: Harvesting and Preparing for Winter

As the vibrant colors of fall take over your garden, it signals a time to reap the rewards of your diligent spring and summer care, but also to start preparing your garden for the colder months ahead. This season of transition is crucial for gardening, especially in a companion planting setup where the interdependence of plants can impact their preparation for winter. Let's explore some essential tasks that will help you maximize your late-season harvests and ensure your garden's resilience through the winter.

Harvesting Late-Season Crops

Late fall is a bountiful time for gardeners, with many crops reaching their peak just before the first frost. Vegetables like pumpkins, squash, Brussels sprouts, and root crops such as carrots and beets are all ready for harvest during this time. Timing is critical when harvesting these crops; too early, and you miss maximizing their flavor and size; too late, and a hard frost could damage them. For root vegetables, a light frost can actually enhance their sweetness, making them even more delicious. When harvesting, use a gentle touch to avoid damaging the plant structure or disturbing the surrounding plants that might still be maturing. For pumpkins and squash, ensure they have a hard skin before picking them, as this indicates they have matured sufficiently and can be stored longer. Utilizing proper harvesting techniques not only ensures the best quality of your produce but also prepares your plants for their next growth cycle.

In a companion garden, where plants are closely interconnected, observing the effects of removing one plant on its neighbors is important. For instance, removing a large squash plant may suddenly expose a neighboring lettuce to more sunlight than it is accustomed to, which could cause it to bolt or wither if not managed correctly. Consider this as you plan your harvest, perhaps providing temporary shade with garden fabric or planning a staggered harvest to minimize the impact on the garden ecosystem.

Preparing Perennials for Winter

Your perennial plants, which will return year after year, require special attention as they prepare to go dormant over winter. This preparation is key to their survival and vigor in the following spring. Begin by gradually reducing water as the weather cools, which helps them harden off and prepares them for winter dormancy. However, ensure the soil isn't completely dry, as they still need moisture to sustain their roots through the winter.

Adding a layer of organic mulch around your perennials can provide them with the necessary insulation from freezing temperatures. Materials like straw, shredded leaves, or bark chips are excellent for this purpose. They not only keep the soil temperature more stable but also add organic matter to the soil as they decompose over time. Be cautious not to mulch too early in the fall; wait until after the first hard freeze, as mulching too soon can trap warmth in the soil, potentially encouraging continued growth that would be vulnerable to sudden dips in temperature.

For companion plants that are sensitive to severe cold, consider installing frost cloths or a cold frame to offer extra protection. These structures can be particularly beneficial in a companion planting setup where delicate herbs or flowers may be interplanted with hardier shrubs or perennials, providing a microclimate that helps all varieties of plants in that bed withstand the cold better.

Planting Cover Crops

One of the most effective strategies for preparing your soil for winter while also setting the stage for spring is planting cover crops. These plants, such as crimson clover, winter rye, or Austrian winter peas, perform multiple functions: they prevent soil erosion, improve soil fertility by fixing nitrogen, and enhance soil structure through their root systems. As they grow, cover crops also suppress weeds and provide habitat for beneficial insects, maintaining the biodiversity in your garden even in the off-season.

Choosing the right cover crops for your companion garden involves considering what will be planted in the area come spring. For example, if you plan to plant heavy feeders like tomatoes or peppers, planting a nitrogen-fixing cover crop such as clover in the fall can enrich the soil with the nutrients these plants will need. Once spring arrives, simply cut down the cover crop and till it into the soil a few weeks before planting your spring crops, which allows it to decompose and release nutrients back into the soil.

Mulching for Winter Protection

As you tidy your garden and remove spent annuals, applying a new layer of mulch can help protect both the soil and any remaining plants during winter. Choose a mulch that not only insulates the ground from freezing temperatures but also will enrich the soil as it breaks down. Organic mulches like wood chips or leaf mold are ideal, as they add structure to the soil and support the activity of earthworms and other beneficial soil organisms.

When applying mulch, especially around young plants or perennials, be careful not to pile it directly against plant stems or crowns, as this can lead to rot. Instead, leave a small gap around the base of the plants to ensure proper air circulation. This practice is especially important in a companion planting setup, where different plants may have varying requirements for mulch depending on their size and growth habits.

By carefully managing these fall tasks, you not only maximize your garden's productivity at the end of the growing season but also protect and enhance your garden's health through the winter. This thoughtful preparation ensures that your garden will emerge from the cold months ready for another fruitful year, continuing the cycle of growth and renewal that makes gardening such a rewarding endeavor.

10.4   Winter Planning and Preparation for Next Season

As the chill of winter begins to make its presence felt, your garden might look like it's settling down for a long rest, yet for you, the gardener, this period is rich with potential for planning and enhancement. Winter is a perfect time to reflect, maintain, and prepare, turning what could be a dormant season into a productive phase for setting the stage for next year's growth.

Reflecting on the Past Season

One of the most valuable habits you can cultivate as a gardener is keeping a detailed garden journal. This practice not only serves as a repository of what you've planted and when but also as a critical tool for reflection. Throughout the growing season, your garden has told stories of triumphs and challenges—perhaps the tomatoes thrived next to basil, offering you a bountiful harvest, or the marigolds didn't quite keep the aphids at bay as hoped. Recording these observations can provide invaluable insights that guide your future garden plans. Note everything from weather patterns to pest invasions, and how different companion plantings fared. Did certain plant combinations seem to deter pests effectively? How did the garden respond to weather extremes? Answering these questions can help refine your strategies, ensuring each season builds on the lessons of the last.

Winter Garden Maintenance

With the garden largely at rest, winter is the ideal time to turn your attention to maintenance tasks that can get overlooked during the busier growing months. Start with your gardening tools, which are essential companions in your gardening endeavors. Cleaning, sharpening, and oiling tools like pruners, spades, and hoes can extend their life and make your gardening more efficient come spring. This is also an opportune time to inspect and repair garden structures such as trellises, raised beds, and greenhouses. Look for signs of wear or damage and make necessary repairs to ensure they're sturdy and ready for another year of supporting your garden's growth. Additionally, cleaning out bird feeders and bird baths can support local wildlife, which plays a vital role in the ecosystem of your garden.

Early Planning for Spring

While the landscape outside may be frosty and still, inside, you can begin to lay the groundwork for your spring garden. Early planning involves several key activities that set the stage for a successful growing season. Start by reviewing your garden journal and seed inventories. Make a list of seeds you need to order, considering both successes from the past season and new varieties you might want to try. Planning your garden layout is also crucial; decide where you will rotate crops to prevent soil depletion and reduce pest buildup. Consider how companion planting will be integrated into this year's garden—perhaps you'll try new combinations based on your reflections from last season. Ordering seeds early can ensure you get the best selection and have everything ready for starting seeds indoors or direct sowing once the weather warms.

Protecting Vulnerable Plants

As winter sets in, some of your garden plants might need a little extra help to survive the cold. Particularly vulnerable plants, such as young perennials, newly planted shrubs, or those that are marginally hardy in your zone, may require protection. Techniques such as mulching with straw or leaves can provide insulation from cold temperatures. For particularly tender plants, consider using burlap wraps or frost cloths that can shield plants from biting winds and frost, yet are breathable enough to prevent moisture buildup, which can lead to fungal diseases. Additionally, providing a windbreak with burlap or similar material around your garden beds can help reduce the drying and damaging effects of cold winter winds on both plants and soil.

As you engage in these winter activities, you are not just passing the time until spring; you are actively enhancing the foundation of your garden. This thoughtful preparation ensures that, as the seasons turn, your garden is ready to emerge stronger, more resilient, and more productive, thanks to the care and planning you invested during the quieter months. This readiness not only sets the stage for a successful spring but also deepens your connection to the natural cycle of growth and renewal, enriching your experience as a gardener.

As we close this chapter on winter preparation, we look forward to the renewal that spring brings. The cold months are not just a time for your garden to rest but also a time for you to plan, prepare, and envision the lush days ahead. The efforts you make now lay the groundwork for a vibrant spring filled with growth and abundance.

Chapter 11:
Expanding Your Knowledge

A S YOU VENTURE DEEPER INTO the world of gardening, the thrill of discovery never seems to wane. Each seed and each plant brings a new opportunity to learn and grow. But beyond the well-trodden paths of traditional gardening lie the exotic alleys—the unusual and the untried. This part of your gardening adventure invites you to experiment with novel plant pairings, some of which may not only surprise you with their compatibility but also with their spectacular contributions to your garden's health and yield. Imagine introducing a plant from across the world into your garden and discovering it has the potential to dramatically improve the growth of your local plants. Such is the potential when you begin to explore exotic and unusual plant pairings.

11.1   Experimenting with Exotic and Unusual Plant Pairings

Exploring New Combinations

One of the most exhilarating aspects of gardening is the freedom to experiment. When you start mixing exotic or less common plants with your usual favorites, you're not just gardening; you're embarking on a botanical adventure. Consider, for example, the possibilities of introducing African marigolds into your vegetable garden. Not only do they bring a vibrant splash of color, but their strong scent is also excellent at deterring pests, making them a perfect companion for your vegetables. Or think about incorporating some Asian greens like bok choy or tatsoi, which can be grown close to your regular lettuce or spinach, offering a delightful contrast in texture and flavor while thriving under similar conditions.

The key to successful experimentation in your garden is understanding the specific needs and growth habits of these exotic plants. This means considering their light, water, and soil preferences, and how these might align with or differ from the plants you already grow. Some exotic plants might require more sunlight or more acidic soil conditions than your local plants, so placing them appropriately within your garden is crucial to ensure all plants thrive.

Understanding Plant Needs

Before introducing an exotic plant into your garden, a thorough research phase is essential. This doesn't just help in understanding the basic care requirements of the plant, but also how it interacts with others. For instance, if you're considering adding some herbs from the Mediterranean region, knowing that they generally prefer well-drained soil and plenty of sun will allow you to place them in your garden where they won't just survive, but thrive alongside companions that share similar needs, such as lavender or thyme.

Moreover, it's important to consider the ecological impact of introducing non-native plants into your garden. Ensure that the species are not invasive in your region and that they will not disrupt local biodiversity. Consulting with local gardening experts or extension services can provide you with the necessary insights to make informed decisions.

Documenting Experiments

Keeping a detailed garden journal or video log becomes invaluable when you start experimenting with new plant pairings. Document everything from your planting strategy to the growth progress and any notable changes in both the new and existing plants. This record-keeping will not only help you track what works and what doesn't but also serve as a precious resource for future gardening endeavors. For instance, noting that the introduction of a certain tropical flower led to an increase in pollinator visits helps you make more informed choices about plant pairings in the future.

Learning from Failure

Not every experiment in your garden will be a success, and that's perfectly okay. Each failure is rich with lessons. Did a new plant pairing result in unexpected plant competition or pest attraction? Analyze what might have gone wrong and adjust your approach accordingly. Maybe the exotic herb you planted requires more shade than anticipated, or perhaps it's not compatible with the native soil type. Adjustments and adaptations are all part of the gardening process.

11.2 The Role of Permaculture Principles in Companion Planting

Permaculture is a gardening philosophy that embodies the essence of working in harmony with nature, creating systems that are sustainable and self-sufficient. At its core, permaculture isn't just about planting; it's about creating ecosystems. It incorporates a set of ethics and principles that guide you to design not only your garden but also your lifestyle, aligning with nature's patterns and cycles. This holistic approach can greatly enhance companion planting by fostering diversity, enhancing soil health, and creating more resilient garden ecosystems.

When you integrate permaculture principles into your companion planting strategy, you begin by observing and interacting with your garden. This means taking time to understand the natural processes and flows in your garden space—how the sun moves, where the water flows, which areas are windy, and what native plants and animals inhabit the space. This deep understanding allows you to design your garden layout in a way that maximizes these natural advantages while minimizing waste and effort. For instance, by placing taller plants in the west to provide afternoon shade for more heat-sensitive plants, or by designing a garden bed that slopes gently south to capture more sunlight and drainage, you're using permaculture design principles to enhance the growth and synergy of your companion plants.

Creating Plant Guilds

One of the most exciting aspects of merging permaculture with companion planting is the creation of plant guilds. A plant guild is essentially a community of plants that closely support each other's growth and survival, mimicking the diversity of natural ecosystems. Each plant in a guild contributes different functions, such as attracting beneficial insects, providing nutrients, or offering shade and support. For example, a simple guild might include a fruit tree surrounded by a nitrogen-fixing legume to enrich the soil, a deep-rooted herb to bring up nutrients from below, and a ground-cover plant to retain moisture and suppress weeds.

To effectively create a plant guild, start with a central element, usually a key plant or tree, and think about what it needs to thrive—such as nitrogen, pest control, or physical support. Then, select companion plants that can provide these benefits. For example, around an apple tree, you might plant daffodils to deter rodents, clover to fix nitrogen, and comfrey to mine minerals from the soil. Not only does this approach make your garden more productive and less labor-intensive, but it also creates a vibrant, multi-layered habitat that supports a wide range of wildlife.

Permaculture Practices for Soil Health

The health of the soil is paramount in permaculture and companion planting. Healthy soil leads to healthy plants, which are more capable of resisting pests and diseases and are more productive. Permaculture encourages several practices to build and maintain healthy soil. One fundamental technique is sheet mulching—layering organic materials directly on the soil, which then decompose to create rich, fertile earth. This method not only improves soil structure and nutrient content but also suppresses weeds and conserves moisture, creating ideal conditions for plant roots to thrive.

Another permaculture practice is the use of dynamic accumulators—plants that gather certain minerals or nutrients from the soil and make them available to other plants. These are often used in companion planting guilds. For instance, planting yarrow can enhance the availability of phosphorus in the soil, which is beneficial for nearby fruiting plants. Similarly, growing deep-rooted plants like borage or chicory can help bring up nutrients from deeper soil layers, making them accessible to shallower-rooted companions.

Incorporating these permaculture principles into your companion planting not only enriches your garden but also aligns your gardening practice with a sustainable and ethical approach to interacting with the natural world. It transforms gardening from a mere hobby into a meaningful contribution to your local environment, promoting biodiversity and resilience. As you continue to apply these principles, you'll likely discover that your garden isn't just a space for growing plants—it's a vibrant ecosystem that nurtures and sustains a rich variety of life, including your own.

11.3   Biointensive Methods for Small-Scale Gardens

Biointensive gardening is a method that focuses on achieving maximum yields from minimal space, making it an ideal technique for urban gardeners or those with limited garden areas. This approach is not only space-efficient but also environmentally sustainable, emphasizing soil health and resource conservation. When combined with companion planting, biointensive methods can significantly enhance the productivity and health of your garden.

At the heart of bio-intensive gardening is the concept of double-digging, where the soil is prepared to a depth of two spade lengths to create a deep, aerated planting bed. This deep soil preparation is crucial because it allows plant roots to penetrate more deeply into the ground, accessing more nutrients and water, thus supporting healthier, more vigorous plant growth. This method also improves drainage and helps break up compacted soil, which is often a challenge in urban settings where soil quality may be poor. When implementing this technique, it's important to add plenty of organic matter, such as compost or well-rotted manure, into the excavated soil. This not only enriches the soil with nutrients but also enhances its structure, increasing its ability to retain moisture and resist erosion.

In the realm of companion planting, integrating biointensive methods means carefully selecting plant combinations that maximize the use of space and complement each other's growth habits and nutrient needs. For example, tall plants like tomatoes can be paired with shorter, shade-tolerant herbs like basil, which benefits from the dappled shade provided by the tomato plants, reducing water stress and sun scorch in hotter climates. Another effective pairing could be carrots and onions; the strong scent of onions can deter carrot fly, while the feathery foliage of carrots provides a living mulch, reducing weed growth around the onion bulbs. This strategic pairing not only maximizes the use of vertical and horizontal space but also creates a microclimate and pest control system that reduces the need for artificial inputs.

Deep soil preparation and thoughtful plant pairing in biointensive companion planting not only optimize the productivity of each square foot of your garden but also create a more resilient growing environment. Plants in such setups tend to be healthier and more robust, capable of resisting pests and diseases more effectively and producing more bountiful harvests. This approach, therefore, is not just about growing more in less space; it's about creating a sustainable, self-reinforcing system where each element of the garden contributes to the whole.

Sustainable watering techniques are another cornerstone of bio-intensive gardening, especially crucial in small-scale gardens where space constraints can affect soil moisture levels. In such gardens, conventional watering methods can be inefficient and wasteful. Instead, bio-intensive gardens benefit significantly from the use of drip irrigation systems, which deliver water directly to the base of the plants at a controlled rate. This method minimizes water wastage through evaporation and runoff and ensures that water reaches the deep roots created by the double-digging method, promoting better growth and reducing water stress during dry periods.

Additionally, the use of mulching in a bio-intensive garden cannot be overstated. Organic mulches, such as straw, leaf mold, or grass clippings, not only keep the soil moist and cool but also gradually decompose and add nutrients back into the soil. This practice supports the biointensive focus on building and maintaining fertile, healthy soil. It also prevents soil compaction from heavy rains or irrigation, maintaining the loose, aerated structure that is vital for root growth and microbial activity.

By implementing these bio-intensive practices, you can transform your small garden space into a highly productive, sustainable ecosystem. The deep, fertile soil you create supports robust plant growth, the strategic plant pairings reduce pest and disease pressure, and the efficient use of water ensures that your garden thrives even in less-than-ideal conditions. As you continue to refine these techniques, your garden becomes not just a source of fresh, healthy produce but also a model of environmental sustainability, demonstrating that even the smallest spaces can have a significant positive impact on the planet.

11.4   Incorporating Aquaponics and Hydroponics with Companion Planting

As you widen your gardening horizons, exploring methods like aquaponics and hydroponics can be a game-changer, especially in environments where traditional soil-based gardening faces limitations. Aquaponics combines aquaculture (raising fish) and hydroponics (growing plants without soil), creating a symbiotic environment where the waste produced by fish supplies nutrients for plants, which in turn purifies the water for the fish. Hydroponics, on the other hand, involves growing plants in nutrient-rich water solutions, eliminating the need for soil altogether. Both systems offer remarkable efficiency in resource use, such as water and space, making them ideal for urban settings or areas with poor soil quality.

The integration of companion planting principles into these water-based systems can enhance their efficiency and biological diversity. In traditional gardens, companion planting promotes beneficial interactions between plants. Similarly, in aquaponics and hydroponics, certain plants can be paired to optimize nutrient uptake and space utilization, enhancing overall system productivity. For instance, leafy greens like lettuce can be grown alongside herbs such as basil in the same hydroponic unit. The basil acts as a natural pest repellent, safeguarding the lettuce, which in return provides shade, maintaining a cooler root environment that benefits the basil during high temperatures.

Managing nutrients in these closed-water systems is critical for maintaining healthy plant and fish life. In aquaponics, the choice and quantity of fish feed directly influence the nutrient composition of the water, which affects plant health. Balancing these elements requires regular monitoring of water quality parameters such as nitrogen levels, pH, and oxygen content. Adjustments might include modifying fish feed or adding supplemental nutrients to support specific plant needs. In hydroponics, nutrient solutions must be carefully formulated and regularly replenished to meet plant requirements. This involves calculating the right concentrations of minerals and nutrients based on the types of plants being grown and their stages of development.

Despite their benefits, integrating companion planting into aquaponics and hydroponics presents unique challenges. One common issue is the different growth rates and nutrient needs of plants, which can complicate their management in a shared water system. For example, fruiting plants like tomatoes require higher levels of nutrients compared to leafy greens, which might lead to nutrient imbalances if grown together. To address this, you can segment the system into zones, each tailored to accommodate plants with similar nutritional and environmental needs. Another challenge is the potential for root crowding in the confined spaces of hydroponic containers, which can hinder plant growth. Regular pruning and careful spacing of plant placements can help manage this issue effectively.

The integration of companion planting with aquaponics and hydroponics not only maximizes the productivity of these innovative systems but also contributes to sustainable urban agriculture practices. By carefully selecting plant combinations that enhance each other's growth and addressing the unique challenges of nutrient management and spatial planning, you can create a highly efficient, self-sustaining system that provides fresh produce right from your balcony or backyard.

As this chapter closes, we reflect on the fascinating possibilities that aquaponics and hydroponics offer to companion planting enthusiasts. These water-based systems represent the cutting edge of horticultural innovation, providing efficient and sustainable methods of food production. The principles discussed here not only deepen your understanding of plant interactions but also empower you to apply these insights in more technologically advanced gardening setups. As we move forward, the knowledge gained sets a solid foundation for exploring further specialized gardening techniques that emphasize sustainability and productivity.

Chapter 12:
Building a Community Around Companion Planting

THINK OF YOUR GARDEN not just as a collection of plants, but as a living network, connecting you with other garden enthusiasts who share your passion for nurturing the earth. This vision can blossom into reality through the creation of a local companion planting group, transforming individual gardening efforts into a collaborative force that enriches your community.

12.1   Join a Local Companion Planting Group

Benefits of Community Gardening

The idea of community gardening, particularly with a focus on companion planting, offers a wealth of benefits that extend far beyond the harvest of your crops. One of the most profound advantages is the pooling of collective knowledge. Each gardener brings their unique set of experiences, successes, and lessons learned, creating a rich repository of wisdom from which all members can draw. This shared learning environment accelerates everyone's gardening skills and can lead to more successful, bountiful gardens.

Moreover, community gardens foster a sense of belonging and connection. They become a place where relationships grow alongside plants, rooted in shared interests and mutual goals. For you, as a beginner, this can be incredibly reassuring—there's always someone to turn to with questions or to offer encouragement when your plants don't behave as expected. Additionally, such groups can significantly impact the local environment. Collective efforts in organic gardening and companion planting contribute to biodiversity, improve air and soil quality, and promote sustainable living practices within your community.

Attending Meetups and Workshops

To tap into these benefits, consider attending regular meetups and workshops. These gatherings tend to be informal—they present a chance to share recent gardening experiences and swap tips—but some can be more structured, with planned activities or guest speakers who specialize in certain aspects of gardening.

Workshops can cover a range of topics relevant to companion planting, from the basics of soil health and plant compatibility to more advanced techniques like pest management and crop rotation. Practical, hands-on sessions, such as seed swaps or planting days, not only enhance learning but also build communal bonds. To attend such events, you might need a small budget for things such as membership fees, but this tends to be money well spent when considering the resources available for exchange within such groups.

Collaborative Garden Projects

Embarking on collaborative garden projects can be one of the most rewarding activities of your gardening group. These projects might involve revitalizing public spaces, creating a community vegetable garden, or even starting a green initiative at local schools. Each project allows you to apply companion planting principles on a larger scale, seeing firsthand how different plants benefit from being grown together.

These projects not only beautify and benefit the community but also serve as public demonstrations of the effectiveness and environmental benefits of companion planting. They can spark interest and inspire others in your community to consider gardening as a viable, enjoyable pursuit.

Using Social Media for Networking

In today's digital age, social media is a powerful tool for building and connecting communities, and your gardening group should not overlook its potential. Platforms like Facebook, Instagram, and Pinterest are perfect for sharing photos of your garden, posting event updates, and exchanging tips with a broader audience. Creating a group or page for your community allows members to stay connected, share successes, and seek advice conveniently.

Beyond local networking, social media platforms can connect you with international companion planting and gardening communities, where you can discover new ideas, trends, and inspirations that can be adapted to your local conditions. This global connection not only enriches your own gardening practices but also brings a wealth of new perspectives and practices that can be shared within your local group.

Note: If this sounds like something you'd be keen to explore, I'd love to see you inside my own Facebook group (Jeff Tucker Homesteading). You can find it at:
https://www.facebook.com/groups/jefftuckerhomesteading

12.2 Sharing Your Companion Planting Successes and Failures

Sharing your experiences in the garden, both the triumphs and the setbacks, is not just about storytelling; it's a crucial part of learning and community building. Every gardener, whether novice or experienced, encounters unique challenges and moments of joy. By opening up about these experiences, you provide insights that can guide others, helping them navigate similar challenges and encouraging them to try new techniques, such as companion planting.

The act of sharing also demystifies the process of gardening. It breaks down the notion that successful gardening is only about perfect outcomes. Instead, it highlights gardening as a process of continuous learning and adaptation. For instance, you might have had great success with tomatoes and basil thriving together, deterring pests and enhancing each other's growth. Sharing this success could inspire another gardener to try companion planting for the first time. Conversely, if you face challenges, such as marigolds failing to deter aphids as expected, discussing these issues can spark conversations about alternative natural pest control methods or adjustments to planting strategies.

Creating a garden blog or vlog is an excellent way to document and share your companion planting journey, even if it's just for you to look back on and marvel at how far you've come. On the other hand, this digital diary might also serve as a detailed resource for others, showcasing what you've planted, how you've arranged your garden, and what the outcomes have been over time. It's not just about posting successes; include your learning moments, how you adjusted your strategies, and what you plan to try next. This approach not only makes your content relatable but also educational.

For example, a vlog entry might give a tour of your garden at peak season, showing the lush growth and discussing the companion planting principles applied. Another post could detail a challenge, like unexpected pest invasions, and follow up with how you addressed it, perhaps by introducing beneficial insects or adjusting plant pairings. These real-time, visual stories can be incredibly engaging and informative, making the concept of companion planting vivid and accessible.

Participating in online gardening forums is another way to engage with a community of like-minded individuals. These platforms allow you to ask questions, share advice, and exchange experiences with people from around the world. Whether it's a question about which plants pair well in a specific climate or seeking advice on organic pest control solutions, these forums can offer a wealth of information and support. When you contribute to these discussions, you're not just learning; you're also helping to build a collective knowledge base that can empower others in their gardening practices.

Attending or even hosting garden tours can be a wonderful way to bring the community together and show the practical applications of companion planting. Invite fellow gardeners, friends, and neighbors to see your garden first-hand. During these tours, you can learn how different plant combinations work together, discuss what you've learned, and share tips for companion planting. This hands-on experience can be incredibly impactful, turning abstract concepts into tangible examples that visitors can see and touch. It also offers a chance for in-person discussion, which can foster a deeper understanding and spark enthusiasm for sustainable gardening practices.

Each of these activities not only enriches your own gardening experience but also strengthens the broader gardening community. By sharing your successes and failures, creating educational content, participating in discussions, and opening your garden to visitors, you help cultivate a more informed, connected, and enthusiastic network of gardeners. This community, in turn, becomes a powerful resource for everyone involved, promoting more sustainable, productive, and enjoyable gardening practices through the collective wisdom and experience of its members.

12.3   Companion Planting Resources and Continuing Education

Immersing yourself in the verdant world of companion planting not only enhances your garden's productivity and beauty but also opens up a realm of continuous learning and community connection. As you delve deeper into this practice, you'll find an abundance of resources that can help expand your knowledge and refine your skills. From insightful books and dynamic online courses to engaging workshops and vibrant gardening communities, the opportunities for growth are as plentiful as seeds in a pod.

Recommended Reading and Resources

Embarking on your gardening path with a well-curated list of books and online resources can significantly enrich your understanding and execution of companion planting. Consider starting with titles like *Carrots Love Tomatoes* by Louise Riotte or *The Vegetable Gardener's Bible* by Edward C. Smith, which are staples in the gardening community for their practical advice and easy-to-follow guidelines. These books not only provide foundational knowledge but also delve into the nuances of plant relationships, offering insights into the specific benefits and challenges of various plant pairings.

In addition to books, numerous websites serve as excellent platforms for both novice and experienced gardeners. Websites like the Old Farmer's Almanac provide a treasure trove of gardening tips, planting calendars, and detailed guides on hundreds of plant species. For a more interactive experience, platforms like Garden.org offer forums where you can ask questions and share experiences with fellow gardeners. These websites often feature articles and blogs by horticulture experts, which can keep you updated on the latest research and trends in companion planting.

12.4 The Future of Companion Planting: Trends and Innovations

As we look towards the horizon of gardening, the future of companion planting is vibrant and full of potential, marked by exciting trends and innovations that promise to revolutionize how we interact with our gardens. The integration of new technologies and forward-thinking garden designs is not just changing the landscape of companion planting but also enhancing our ability to produce food sustainably and securely on a global scale.

Emerging Trends in Companion Planting

One of the most intriguing trends in companion planting is the increasing use of data-driven insights to optimize plant interactions. Gardeners and researchers are now using sophisticated algorithms to analyze vast amounts of data on plant characteristics and their interactions. This approach allows for the creation of highly customized companion planting schemes that are maximized for efficiency, yield, and sustainability. Imagine knowing precisely which plant combinations will thrive in your specific garden environment based on real-time data analysis. This level of precision not only enhances garden productivity but also minimizes waste and maximizes the use of available resources.

Another emerging trend is the concept of vertical companion planting, where vertical gardens are designed to take advantage of the vertical space in urban environments. This method allows for the close proximity of companion plants that benefit from being stacked vertically, such as strawberries and peas. The peas climb upward, providing shade and moisture retention for the strawberries below, while the strawberries spread out across the ground, suppressing weeds and maintaining soil moisture. This efficient use of space is particularly valuable in urban areas, where horizontal space may be limited.

Innovations in Garden Design

Innovative garden design is rapidly evolving, particularly with the integration of companion planting principles into new and unconventional spaces. One such innovation is the development of modular garden systems, which allow individuals to easily swap out plants based on seasonal needs and companion planting requirements. These systems can be adjusted for variables such as sunlight exposure, water needs, and soil conditions, making it easier than ever to create dynamic, responsive gardening setups that evolve throughout the year.

Another design innovation involves the use of companion planting in public and communal spaces to create self-sustaining ecosystems that provide aesthetic, environmental, and food-producing benefits. For example, city parks and rooftops are being transformed into lush gardens where companion plants help control pests, improve soil health, and provide fresh produce to the community. This not only beautifies urban environments but also brings fresh food closer to where people live, reducing food transportation costs and associated carbon footprints.

The Role of Technology in Gardening

Technology is playing an increasingly significant role in companion planting by providing tools that help gardeners make more informed decisions. Gardening apps have become particularly popular, offering features that help plan and manage gardens with precision. These apps can advise on the best plant pairings, remind you of the best times to water and fertilize, and even provide weather alerts to help protect your plants from adverse conditions. The use of drones and satellite imaging is also on the rise, providing large-scale farmers with detailed views of their fields to manage companion planting effectively at scale.

Precision agriculture tools are another technological advancement that is making a big impact. These tools allow for the precise application of water, nutrients, and natural pesticides, dramatically increasing the efficiency of resource use. For companion planting, this means being able to deliver exactly what each plant needs without waste, ensuring that all plants in the garden thrive together.

Sustainability and Global Food Security

Perhaps most importantly, the advancements in companion planting are playing a crucial role in promoting sustainability and enhancing global food security. By maximizing the natural benefits of plant relationships, companion planting reduces the need for chemical inputs, lowers water usage, and increases crop diversity. This not only makes gardening more sustainable but also contributes to global food security by demonstrating how diverse planting strategies can lead to more resilient food systems.

As these trends and innovations continue to unfold, the future of companion planting looks promising. The integration of technology, innovative design, and sustainable practices is paving the way for more efficient, productive, and environmentally friendly gardening methods. These advancements not only enhance the individual gardener's experience but also contribute to broader environmental goals, helping to create a more sustainable and food-secure world.

Final Thoughts

A S WE NEAR THE END of our journey through the vibrant world of companion planting (for now, at least!), let's take a moment to reflect on the core principles and transformative insights we've explored. We began with the simple yet profound understanding that plants, much like people, thrive in supportive communities. This book has unveiled the intricate relationships between plants, demonstrating how thoughtful pairings can enhance garden yield, naturally manage pests, and improve the health of your soil. These relationships underscore the importance of biodiversity and illustrate the substantial sustainability benefits of companion planting.

From the initial steps as beginners, you have now traversed through foundational knowledge to advanced gardening strategies, empowering you with the confidence to maximize your garden's potential. Whether you have a small urban balcony or a sprawling rural backyard, the techniques and concepts we've discussed are adaptable to gardens of all sizes and settings. Your newfound knowledge equips you to tailor these practices to your own climate and local conditions, ensuring that you can apply what you've learned, no matter where you garden.

One of the most significant themes explored in this book is the profound environmental impact of adopting organic gardening practices. By choosing to garden organically, you contribute to reducing chemical use, enhancing local biodiversity, and promoting ecological health. Remember, each plant you nurture organically helps to support a healthier planet.

However, the journey doesn't end here. I encourage you to continue expanding your knowledge about companion planting and organic gardening, just as I have done since being a young boy in my grandad's allotment. Join local gardening groups, engage in online forums, and participate in workshops. These communities offer invaluable opportunities for learning and can deepen your understanding and appreciation of gardening.

I also urge you to experiment in your garden. Try new plant combinations, innovate with different layouts, and observe the results. Share your experiences, both successes and challenges, with fellow gardeners. Each experiment, each season, enriches your understanding and hones your skills in companion planting.

Now, as we part ways in this book, I call upon you to apply these principles and techniques to create your own thriving, sustainable garden. Consider the broader impact of your gardening choices and strive for practices that not only benefit your household but also contribute positively to our environment.

As you continue to grow as a gardener, remember that you are not just cultivating plants, but you are also a steward of the earth. Each choice you make in your garden resonates within the larger tapestry of our ecological system. With every plant that thrives in your care, you are part of a global movement towards sustainability and balance.

Thank you for joining me on this green journey. May your gardens flourish and your spirits soar as you sow and nurture not just plants but a sustainable future. Here's to growing together, learning endlessly, and building a world where gardens are not only places of beauty and bounty but also bastions of ecological harmony. Happy gardening!

And don't forget to join me in the Facebook group: (https://www.facebook.com/groups/jefftuckerhomesteading)

References

1. *10 Ways Cover Crops Enhance Soil Health—SARE*
    https://www.sare.org/publications/cover-crops/ecosystem-services/10-ways-cover-crops-enhance-soil-health/
2. *12 Plants That Repel Unwanted Bugs—Treehugger*
    https://www.treehugger.com/plants-that-repel-unwanted-insects-4864336
3. *15 Companion Planting Mistakes to Avoid This Season*
    https://www.epicgardening.com/companion-planting-mistakes/
4. *20 Ways to Boost Soil Fertility*
    https://rodaleinstitute.org/blog/20-ways-to-boost-soil-fertility/
5. *30 Essential Pollinator Plants for Your Garden*
    https://www.gardendesign.com/plants/pollinators.html
6. *A Comprehensive Guide for Succession Planting in The ...*
    https://www.epicgardening.com/succession-planting/
7. *An In-Depth Companion Planting Guide*
    https://www.motherearthnews.com/organic-gardening/companion-planting-guide-zmaz81mjzraw/
8. *Attracting Pollinators to Your Garden Using Native Plants*
    https://www.fs.usda.gov/wildflowers/pollinators/documents/attractingPollinatorsV5.pdf
9. *Beneficial Insects in the Garden*
    https://www.almanac.com/beneficial-insects-garden
10. *Benefits of Cover Crops—SARE*
    https://www.sare.org/publications/managing-cover-crops-profitably/benefits-of-cover-crops/
11. *Biodiversity in residential gardens: a review of the ...*
    https://link.springer.com/article/10.1007/s10531-023-02694-9
12. *Companion Planting Chart and Guide for Vegetable Gardens*
    https://www.almanac.com/companion-planting-guide-vegetables
13. *Companion Planting Chart for India & Benefits*
    https://www.allthatgrows.in/blogs/posts/companion-planting-chart

14. *Companion Planting for Increased Garden Success!* https://northernwildflowers.ca/blogs/our-blog/companion-planting-for-increased-garden-success
15. *Companion Planting for Pest Control* https://journeywithjill.net/gardening/2019/02/26/companion-planting-pest-control/
16. *Companion Planting Reference Guide* https://www.gardentowerproject.com/blogs/learning-center/companion-planting
17. *Companion Planting: Nature's Free Organic Pest Control* https://rethinkrural.raydientplaces.com/blog/companion-planting-chart
18. *Companion Planting | Extension | West Virginia University* https://extension.wvu.edu/lawn-gardening-pests/gardening/garden-management/companion-planting
19. *Container Garden Companion Planting Guide* https://www.permacultureapartment.com/post/container-garden-companion-planting
20. *Crop Rotations* https://rodaleinstitute.org/why-organic/organic-farming-practices/crop-rotations
21. *Efficient Use of Water in the Garden and Landscape* https://aggie-horticulture.tamu.edu/earthkind/drought/efficient-use-of-water-in-the-garden-and-landscape/
22. *How to Hand Pollinate Fruit & Vegetables Guide* https://themicrogardener.com/wp-content/uploads/2016/11/How-to-Hand-Pollinate-Fruit-Vegetables-2.pdf
23. *How Nitrogen-Fixing Plants Can Perk Up Your Garden* https://www.treehugger.com/how-nitrogen-fixing-plants-can-perk-your-garden-4863746
24. *How Nitrogen-Fixing Plants Enrich the Soil—2024* https://www.masterclass.com/articles/how-nitrogen-fixing-plants-enrich-the-soil
25. *How to organize a Plant Swap like a pro!* https://homesteadbrooklyn.com/all/2017/10/12/how-to-organize-a-plant-swap-like-a-pro

26. *How to Test Soil pH With and Without a Kit*
    https://www.thespruce.com/how-to-test-soil-acidity-alkalinity-
    without-a-test-kit-1388584
27. *Hydroponics vs. Aquaponics - A Complete, and Honest ...*
    https://www.trees.com/gardening-and-
    landscaping/hydroponics-vs-aquaponics
28. *Impact of Technology on Organic Farming*
    https://erpnews.com/from-field-to-fork-victoria-gerrard-la-
    crosse-explores-the-impact-of-technology-on-organic-farming/
29. *List of Companion Plants*
    https://en.wikipedia.org/wiki/List_of_companion_plants
30. *Optimizing Sunlight - Deep Roots Project* https://www.deep-
    roots-project.org/grow-your-own-food-all/optimizing-
    sunlight#:~:text=You%20can%20get%20by%20with,full%20sun
    %20in%20mid%20summer.
31. *Pollinator-Friendly Native Plant Lists*
    https://xerces.org/pollinator-conservation/pollinator-friendly-
    plant-lists
32. *Popular Herbs Compatible with Vegetable Plants*
    https://www.bibralakesoils.com.au/popular-herbs-to-pair-with-
    vegetable-plants/
33. *Preparing Garden Soil for Planting*
    https://www.almanac.com/soil-preparation-how-do-you-
    prepare-garden-soil-planting
34. *science-based companion planting: 'plant partners,' with Jessica
    Walliser* https://awaytogarden.com/science-based-companion-
    planting-plant-partners-with-jessica-walliser/
35. *Soak, Drip or Spray How to Choose a Watering System*
    https://www.gardeners.com/how-to/how-to-choose-a-watering-
    system/8747.html
36. *The 12 Permaculture Design Principles*
    https://permacultureprinciples.com/permaculture-principles/
37. *The Benefits of Companion Planting in Your Garden*
    https://www.thehomesteadgarden.com/the-benefits-of-
    companion-planting-in-your-garden/
38. *The Many Benefits of Community Gardens*
    https://www.greenleafcommunities.org/the-many-benefits-of-
    community-gardens/

39. *The Three Sisters of Indigenous American Agriculture*
https://www.nal.usda.gov/collections/stories/three-sisters
40. *Vegetable Companion Plants that Repel Insect Pests - Fafard*
https://fafard.com/vegetable-companion-plants-that-repel-
insect-pests/
41. *What Soil Organic Matter is and What It Does*
https://ahdb.org.uk/knowledge-library/what-soil-organic-
matter-is-and-what-it-does
42. *What You Should Know About Biointensive Gardening - HGTV*
https://www.hgtv.com/outdoors/gardens/biointensive-
gardening-for-abundance